4

Rochester College Lectures on Preaching
Volume 4

Preaching
Hebrews

David Fleer and Dave Bland, editors

Preaching Hebrews

1648 Campus Court
Abilene, TX 79601
www.acupressbooks.com

Copyright © 2003

David Fleer and Dave Bland, editors

Printed in the United States of America

Book Design by Sarah Bales

ISBN 0-89112-138-2

Library of Congress Card Number: 2003105898

Second Edition
06 07 08 09 10 / 6 5 4 3 2

Table of Contents

We express our gratitude to Allen Black, Ron Cox, Brian Faust, Josh Fleer, Spencer Furby, and Jonathan Woodall for their careful reading of the manuscripts in various stages of development; to Jody Fleischhut for her personable work with the Seminar, and to Jim and Caye Randolph for enabling so many of the Seminar's participants.

To the memories of Marvelyn Fleer and Leo and Mabel Perleth, my first community of faith and whose unconditional love sustains me long after their deaths. - David Fleer

To the memories of J. P. Sanders, E. W. McMillan, and Delane Way who, as a young preacher, were my first elders and mentors in the faith and who showed me how to "run with endurance." - Dave Bland

Biographical Sketches

Dave Bland

For more than two decades, Dave Bland has devoted his life to preaching tenures with the Eastside Church of Christ in Portland, Oregon and, currently, with the White Station congregation in Memphis. Dave complements his life's activity in preaching with a background in rhetoric (Ph.D., University of Washington) and has long cultivated an interest in wisdom literature. In addition to teaching and preaching, Dave directs the Doctor of Ministry Program at Harding University Graduate School of Religion.

Charles Campbell

Chuck Campbell's interest in homiletics began while he was serving a six-year pastorate at First Presbyterian Church in Stuttgart, Arkansas. Following that pastorate, Chuck pursued a calling to teach, earning a Ph.D. in theology and ethics at Duke University and taking a position on the Columbia Theological Seminary faculty. His work focuses on the Christological, ecclesiological, and ethical dimensions of preaching.

Richard Eslinger

For more than thirty years a dynamic United Methodist pastor and teacher in a variety of regional and national settings, Dick has sustained both pastoral and scholarly commitment toward the renewal of biblical preaching and liturgical celebration among God's people. He is author of seven books in the field of homiletics, including his latest, *The Web of Preaching*, which interprets current movements in preaching and approaches to homiletic method, especially as they intersect and complement a whole "web." Dick thrives in community life, and presently enjoys his work as Professor of Homiletics and Worship at United Theological Seminary in Dayton, Ohio. He serves frequently as adjunct faculty for the Upper Room Academy for Spiritual Formation in its several expressions around the country. Soaring both as a glider pilot and as a preacher of the Gospel are joyful life vocations.

David Fleer

David Fleer's devotion to preaching first found expression through a long-tenured pulpit ministry with the Vancouver Church of Christ in the state of Washington. His Ph.D. in Speech Communication at the University of Washington moved him into teaching, where he is currently Professor of Religion and Communication at Rochester College. Co-editor of the current series on preaching, David's work is characterized as a thoughtful and passionate attempt to walk afresh in the world of Scripture so that readers and listeners may experience the reality of the Gospel of God.

Luke Timothy Johnson

As the author of numerous books, most notably *Scripture and Discernment* and *The Real Jesus*, reviewers describe Luke Johnson's writing as refreshing, engaging, and eminently readable. Luke teaches New Testament and Christian Origins at Candler School of Theology, Emory University in Atlanta. What makes him so attractive to preachers can partially be understood in the words he wrote in a volume entitled *Faith's Freedom*. "Christian Faith is something to be lived for before it is something to be thought about." His serious scholarship and unapologetic faith make him a model for those who preach Jesus.

Greg Stevenson

Although Greg Stevenson preached for three years at the Marks Church of Christ in Marks, MS, his primary ministry has been in the classroom. After receiving his Ph.D. in New Testament from Emory University, Greg has taught on the religion faculty at Rochester College since 1999. His areas of specialty include Greek, the Book of Revelation, archaeology, and the study of Christianity and popular culture.

Foreword

Thomas G. Long

"Long ago God spoke...."

These are the first words of Hebrews, and one can often tell much about a document by paying close attention to its opening phrases. Indeed, the rest of Hebrews can well be understood as an elaboration of this opening gambit: "Long ago God spoke." God *spoke*? What can that mean? We quickly assure ourselves that no embarrassing literalism is meant here. The author of Hebrews is philosophically sophisticated, a neo-Platonist after all, and when he says "God spoke," he certainly doesn't have in mind any crude anthropomorphisms, like a nursing home God who suddenly blinks his eyes and awakes from a centuries-long coma to utter a few enigmatic words—God spoke!—or a God who parts the skies and, like a neighbor across the backyard fence, chats up mortals about the cosmic news or the weather in heaven—God spoke! No, no, nothing like that. The author of Hebrews, we hasten to explain, is using a metaphor, a symbol. The idea of God speaking is but a poetic way to say that God communicates, gets the message across "in many and various ways"—through the prophets, through deeds of power, and, at last, through a Son (1:1-2).

True enough, but before we allow the image of a speaking God to drift too far off shore into the deeps of metaphor and abstraction, we must face the fact that when Hebrews says "God spoke," part of what is meant is that God really *talks*—through prophets and psalmists and preachers and a thousand different other talkers—and that faith depends on the actual sound of words vibrating in the air and striking the ears. The book of Hebrews crackles with the spoken word—God talks, Scripture talks, believers talk, the church talks, blood talks, Jesus talks. Hebrews tells us that not even death can get the saints to shut up. Old Abel is dead as a doornail, but "through his faith he still speaks" (11:4).

Part of the reason the author of Hebrews is so captivated by the medium of speech is that he is, himself, a preacher, and the book he has produced is actually an "exhortation" (13:22), a sermon. Like all preachers before and since, the author of Hebrews knows that his only resource, his only weapon, his only scalpel, his only lifeline is the spoken word. If the gospel is to be preached and believed, it will not be because of skits, stained glass, PowerPoint™, or praise bands. If faith is to be born, it will come because some preacher climbs into a pulpit somewhere with nothing but the frail vessels of human words, prays like mad that they be filled with the cargo of the Spirit, and launches them across the wide sea of human hearing, hopeful they will find safe harbor in receptive ears. The preacher of Hebrews knows that before faith is kinetic, it is acoustic. Thus, it is fitting that the superb scholarly essays on the book of Hebrews in this volume should be complemented with equally fine sermons, for unless the lines on the page end up as words in the mouth of the preacher, the urgent claim of Hebrews is lost.

The main reason, however, that Hebrews vibrates with the sound of the spoken word is that the preacher believes that the gospel is in dire trouble among his congregation because it has so little to show in the way of results. People in all times and places are prone to seek out religious practices that produce tangible, visible results. Whether it is burning a bull on a remote mountain altar or sliding into the pew at the local Temple of Positive Thinking, people want a religion that pays off in ways one can see—bigger harvests, healthier bodies, securer incomes, or at least a bit more peace of mind on demand. And that, of course, is just the problem with the Christian faith. In the world of religious "Show and Tell," it has so little to show. Other gospels, other philosophies of life can advance your career, sharpen your parenting skills, enhance your personality, help you get ahead. All the Christian faith has to show for itself is a cross to be picked up daily.

But wait, isn't the gospel about God's great victory over all that oppresses human life? Isn't the gospel about the resurrection triumph of life over death? Yes, but the victory, which one day every eye will see, is at present hidden and cannot be glimpsed by the naked eye. As the preacher of Hebrews puts it, "As it is, we do not yet see everything in subjection..." (2:8). What do we see now? We see Jesus trudging up Calvary's hill to defeat; we see a life of faith that leads up the same hill, bearing one another's burdens, all the while blessing those who persecute. No wonder the preacher's congregation had grown weary. No wonder their hands were drooping and their knees were weak (12:12). It is hard to practice a faith where the results are hidden. No wonder many in the congregation had begun to let their worship attendance slacken (10:25), preferring to spend the Lord's Day doing something like tuning in the NFL games, where at least you could see who won.

But if the victory of the gospel cannot be seen, it can be *heard*. The spoken word can take us where the eye cannot go, and faith is "the conviction of things not seen" (11:1). So the preacher of Hebrews climbs into that pulpit and fills the air with the sound of hopeful words. "Long ago God spoke," he told them. "For the sake of joy, Jesus endured the cross," he preached, "disregarding its shame, and has taken his seat at the right hand of God" (12:2). You can't see that? "Well," replied the preacher, "I'm telling you that. Hold fast to what is said. Talk to each other. Exhort one another. When you start to flag in zeal, listen to the encouraging words of those who have run the race before you. You are, after all, surrounded by a great cloud of *talkers* (12:1). I'm telling you the truth: what catches the eye is just the tip of the iceberg and the full story is that what is visible is made from things that are not visible" (11:3).

There is an old Jewish tale about a little group of provincial students who, by begging and pleading, managed to persuade one of the great teachers of Torah to instruct them in the wisdom of Moses. The arrangement was that once each week the great master would travel from the city out to the countryside and would spend the day with the humble students, breaking open to them the great truths of Torah. What a gift, the students thought, to be taught by one so wise in the law of Moses.

But a problem quickly developed. On the very first day of instruction, when the group had gathered in the modest home of one of the students, the wise man began to teach, "And God spoke all these things to Moses, saying...." As soon as he uttered these words, the youngest and least experienced of the students stood up in astonishment, his eyes ablaze with wonder.

"God spoke!" he cried. "God *spoke*!" And the young man began to dance around the room, as if in a trance, shouting over and over in frenzied amazement, "God spoke! God spoke! God spoke!" Finally the other students had to restrain him, and, much embarrassed, they locked him in the woodshed so that the master could continue his teaching.

Week after week, this scene was repeated. "And God spoke all these things to Moses," the old teacher would begin, only to be interrupted by the youngest student pushing away from the table in excitement, whirling around the room exclaiming, "God spoke! God spoke!" Week after week, the lesson could continue only when his brothers had locked him in the woodshed.

Finally when the master had finished his course of teaching Moses, the students were expressing their gratitude. One of them looked at the old teacher and shook his head sadly, "Our only sorrow is that, alas, our youngest brother learned none of the truths of Torah"

"No, no," replied the master. "He learned the greatest truth of Torah: we live in a world where God speaks."

So as we read the chapters of this book, we must, of course, open our eyes. But let us also open our ears, for we live in a world, as the preacher of Hebrews knew, where God speaks.

Thomas G. Long
Bandy Professor of Preaching
Candler School of Theology
Emory University

Introduction
Preaching and the World
Hebrews Imagines
David Fleer

The Rochester College Sermon Seminar and the series of
books it has inspired have been built on the conviction that
Christian preaching today needs revision. Such reforming begins
with a close and faithful reading of Scripture, an engagement so
serious that the world of Scripture ultimately sets agendas and
invents expectations for meaningful life.

In May 2002 preachers came to the Rochester Sermon
Seminar from across the United States and Canada. We
represented a rich diversity in Christian faith: Roman Catholic
and Protestant, from St. Paul's Parish to Emmanuel's House. We
were Presbyterian and Lutheran, Salvation Army and the United
Church of Canada, Methodists and Vineyardians, Baptists and
Disciples, Christian Church, Community Church and Churches
of Christ. We were black and white, male and female, old and
young.

More than 150 of us gathered for one common purpose:
to study Scripture that we might be better equipped to preach
to the people of God to whom we have been called. Our
common conviction was that the Bible is the richest resource
for sustaining life and preaching and is able to lift us past our old
human barriers and labels. United as believers we came to study,
think, talk, prepare, and hope.

We have not always been together. Issues and doctrines
have, in the past, divided us. At our best we have been able
to make light of these erected obstructions, as expressed in the
story that took place sometime between the Second World War

and the second Vatican council. In a small town in Vermont, a Protestant church was badly damaged by fire. The congregation immediately launched a fund raising campaign to erect a new church building. One of the members carried the fund raising so far that he asked the local Roman Catholic priest for a donation.

"Now Harold," said the priest, "You know I can't do a thing like that, give money to build a Protestant church. But," he added, "I will give you $100 to help tear down the old one."[1]

On this occasion, however, we were not divided. For 48 hours we united as believers with open minds and hearts, craving to read Hebrews closely and faithfully and move into the world of Scripture.

In the present volume, too, we wish to grant the book of Hebrews the opportunity to pull all of us into the world it envisions, allowing it the power to judge, convict, and form us into a community God desires. This is not an easy task for several reasons, most notably the fact that the world of Hebrews is quite alien from our own.

This was the theme articulated in Luke Timothy Johnson's opening keynote address, "The World Imagined by Scripture."[2] Faced with a world depicted in Hebrews that is "truly other," Johnson considered three hermeneutic options for us preachers.

First, he said, we could pretend that we are still living in the world of Scripture. Of course, since the Enlightenment, we have had a hard time pulling this off. Modernity is quite different from antiquity and if we assume that the contemporary world is envisioned in Scripture, we are not paying attention and are involved in a "false consciousness."

A second option, attractive especially to those of us trained in the methods of historical critical biblical scholarship, has been to assume the superiority of the Enlightenment. Thus, we

---

[1] This story has appeared in several forms and locations. This rendering is adapted from an appearance in a Spring 2002 issue of *The Christian Century.*

[2] Luke Timothy Johnson, "The World Imagined by Scripture" (Presented to the Fifth Annual Rochester College Sermon Seminar, *Hebrews: The Letter About Hope, The Letter About Home*, Rochester Hills, MI, May 20, 2002).

have approached the world of Hebrews by explaining it away, saying, "We understand how the text came into being and why ancient people thought as they did." Johnson observed, however, that historical critical scholarship has unearthed the world that created the book of Hebrews but in this preoccupation has avoided the world created by Scripture. Understanding the world that created Hebrews, alone, tends to distance that world through objective explanation.

The problem is exacerbated by the limited paradigm the Enlightenment has designed. The Enlightenment trumps the biblical world of faith when it demands that all realities be measured and quantified by what can be seen and touched. The world of Hebrews, of course, operates under a different system. In Hebrews, faith is assumed and claims are judged as real by One whom no one can see. In a world so envisioned, Johnson contends, we must enter imaginatively. Empirical verification is insufficiently equipped for such an assignment.

The third and preferred approach is to engage the world Scripture imagines. We begin, therefore, with a hermeneutic of generosity, which Johnson explained, "[tries] to understand the world imagined by Scripture, not by explaining it, but by understanding it so as to learn from that world and to engage it critically, marking the ways we do or do not live in that world and to discern what that means." We can progress homiletically only if we let go of our preoccupation with the world that produced the Bible and begin to engage the world the Bible produced. This is the preacher's *hermeneutical* task set forth in the Seminar and developed in this volume.

Our consistent belief in this series has been that preaching is rooted in the biblical text and that to speak to the deepest levels of human need we must move into the world of the Bible where there exists a place preachers may invite their congregations to enter. Johnson sets out the creative development of this symbolic world, "The Bible imagines a world created by God and by imagining that world, reveals it, and by revealing it, invites us to enter it, and by inviting us to enter it, enables us to embody it, and by embodying it, makes the world real." Preaching thus involves an imaginative leap where God speaks through Scripture, where "Scripture is infinite in its possibility for meaning," and where the living God continues to work in new ways. *This* is the essential evolution at the heart of the preachers' *homiletical* duty.

Like previous volumes in the Rochester Lectures on Preaching, the current work is divided into two parts. The first is a collection of four related essays meant to orient the reader to the world clearly conceived in Hebrews. The second half appropriates this orientation with sermons for particular Christian congregations.

We have long considered preaching from Hebrews a difficult task. In fact, when assessing passages from which to preach on Jesus, Hebrews usually finishes a distant fifth, trailing all the synoptics and John. Most foreboding is Hebrews' depiction of Jesus and discipleship, images clearly at odds with contemporary Christian beliefs. The opening chapter by Luke Johnson is, therefore, prerequisite reading for anyone preaching Jesus and Christian discipleship. Johnson's essay is a stirring and close reading of Hebrews. From his immersion in the biblical text, Johnson observes that Hebrews avoids easy Christological titles, depicting instead a robust Character whose life, death, and resurrection have fundamentally altered the structures of human existence. Hebrews maintains the paradox of Jesus as fully God and fully human when it speaks of his perfection through suffering, the essential quality that allowed him to progressively grow into his stature as divine son. Similarly, Johnson argues, the suffering described in Hebrews is at the heart of Christian discipleship, which expresses itself in communal caring and opens Jesus' followers to the mystery of God.

In the second chapter Chuck Campbell both complements Johnson's suggestive work and advances his own postliberal homiletic theory. Campbell extends his fundamental corrective of the New Homiletic by carefully examining the axiom that the biblical text should shape the form of the sermon. Campbell argues that Hebrews, a non-narrative sermon based on a narrative text (the story of Jesus), wreaks havoc with this assumption. Campbell carefully explores in Hebrews the complex relationship between narrative text and discursive sermon with implications for both the pulpit and homiletic theory. Campbell finds the preacher of Hebrews a model for those who wish to capture the unity and logic of the story of Jesus without simplistically using narrative form. Campbell argues with clarity that in Hebrews discursive speech can be shaped by the logic of a particular narrative that interprets the concrete situation of the community of faith within the gospel story of Jesus. Campbell's heuristic article solicits theoretical response and courts practical enactment.

Dick Eslinger begins the third chapter with a description of the "pastoral situation" that characterized the communities addressed in Hebrews and the rhetorical strategies available to the preacher. Essential metaphors in Hebrews, which both persuade and make the preacher's argument ever present, include covenant, journey, and rest. With a clear and specific echo of Johnson's call for a communal expression, Eslinger next locates in Hebrews essential virtues that sustain the community on its journey. These include boldness, memory and hospitality. In an exciting conclusion to the essay, Eslinger speaks a word to preachers, placing before our lives the very metaphors that shape those envisioned in Hebrews as well as the lives of our hearers.

The first half of the book concludes with a provocative essay that moves us, by example, toward the sermons. Claiming that the best sermons design a dialogue between the Scripture's world and ours, Greg Stevenson looks to the rock band U2 as a notable example of effective indirect communication. Advising that we neither attack the music nor mine its illustrative material, Stevenson encourages us to give close attention to the ongoing theological conversation occurring in the music of U2. In fact, Stevenson urges us to be a part of the conversation because we may learn something. Specifically, he asks that we note how U2 accomplishes what we preachers strive for, bringing the world of Scripture to bear on our culture. The indirection of the musical message of U2 weaves biblical themes and language into the fabric of their songs. Stevenson locates his research in the song "Walk On," whose words were inspired from Heb 10-12. Here, he argues forcibly that in form, content and function "Walk On" represents a sermon in the shape of a song, encouraging its audience in the same way as Hebrews. This essay's invaluable analysis reveals concrete and creative ways to conceive the sermon.

This volume's seven sermons are an inventive mix from six different preachers who have lived with and preached from the world imagined in Hebrews. Three of the seven sermons come from two preachers in one church, which may necessitate some explanation. John York and Rubel Shelly minister at the Woodmont Hills Church of Christ in Nashville where, each Sunday, they alternate preaching among the three services. Once every few weeks they jointly present a dialogic sermon for each worship event. In September 2002, they began a series of fifteen sermons on Hebrews entitled, "Strength for the Journey." In late December, York wrote,

> Our thinking about the series and excitement for preaching it was strongly shaped by our experiences at the Sermon Seminar in Rochester. The work of Johnson, Campbell, Eslinger and Stevenson opened windows for understanding the world of Hebrews and provided us with wonderful entry points into our contemporary circumstances. We received overwhelming affirmation from the congregation for the series. While the series is now completed, the Hebrews preacher's work has just begun in the lives of our members.[3]

In this context, York's sermon carefully applies Johnson's insights on Hebrews' Christology (Jesus as pioneer) to Christians quite interested in angels. In a very creative conclusion he observes our lives from the viewpoint of one living in the imagined world of Hebrews. Here York effectively accomplishes Johnson's directive that we preachers "mark the ways we do or do not live in the [world of Scripture] and discern what that means."

Characteristically thoughtful and discursive, Shelly takes seriously Hebrews' development of Jesus' character. Focusing specifically on his role as priest, and thus following Campbell's suggestion that this example is at the center of the "logic" of Hebrews, Shelly effectively supports the conviction that suffering is a means of growth in Jesus' life and ours.

---

[3] Email correspondence to the author, December 20, 2002.

Then, Shelly and York work in tandem in one sermon that, I think, captures the rich teaching that can be accomplished in a sustained series. Their choice dialogue allows questions to surface and objections to be honestly probed. This is especially helpful when one is explaining, in Hebrews' case, "To suffer is to learn." The sermon's midcourse interview exemplifies its greatest concern.

In a homily delivered one year after 9/11, Dean Smith casts the dual nature of Jesus as God and human in the complex setting of suffering. Giving close attention to the theological issues articulated in Johnson's chapter and absorbing Eslinger's emphasis of the metaphor of journey, Smith's passionate sermon entwines the call of his text in Hebrews with the new temptations we face. As you read this sermon, pay close attention to the ways it parallels the model Stevenson has found in U2, a creative message enmeshed in the biblical text that has power to shape our stories.

James Thompson has elsewhere argued from Pauline literature that the apostle's dense theological arguments serve as a model for reflective preaching today.[4] Thompson's substantive work parallels Campbell's critique of the New Homiletic and narrative preaching. His sermon "Did Anything Happen," grows out of a life-long journey with Hebrews, aligns with Campbell's essential thesis, and respects the narrative behind the text. Through his language Thompson retains an organic relationship between the meaning of the stories and his discursive sermon. His tensive presentation is an outstanding instance of Campbell's ideal as he invites listeners to participate in the narrative life Hebrews describes.

The most uniquely powerful sermon comes from one who is not a preacher. New Testament professor Ron Cox is known for his passionate love for the biblical text. Few can, or perhaps would even want to, rival Cox's ethos for Heb 4:12-13. What he describes as a line-by-line meditation gives this familiar passage a creative new hearing that honors the bold narratives behind the Hebrews text and the God it describes. This sermon is surely

---

[4] James Thompson, *Preaching Like Paul: Homiletical Wisdom for Today* (Louisville: Westminster John Knox Press, 2001).

the most prophetic in this collection, condemning prooftexting as well as an historical critical approach that treats the Bible "like a dead, inanimate, ancient object." The sermon exposes readers before a sword-bearing God in whose presence we are graciously healed.

One of the presenters at the Seminar was Ross Thomson, who preaches for the North Lake Church of Christ, near Atlanta. Thomson helped participants creatively explore, through his own work, the homiletic possibilities from the rich resources of the Seminar. In the final sermon in this volume, Thomson works with the metaphor of journey and its tension set against the virtues of boldness, memory and hope. Using two passages in Hebrews, Thomson draws upon extensive literary resources and lays out the issues located in the world of Hebrews as they appear in the lives of his Georgia congregation.

At the 2002 Seminar we talked about Hebrews, theology, praxis, and preaching. Our experience was framed with worship. Symbolizing our unity of spirit, we closed the conference with a communion service, *koinonia*. After working together in Scripture, we shared a common meal, expressing our common dependence on God and union in God's pursuit of us in Scripture. Thus, the Seminar, born in a healthy ecumenical environment, has now evolved into a text that is published in one Christian fellowship but, we hope, will have a larger overhearing audience. Now, may this volume help to create in us a preaching imagination that will allow us to experience and preach this reality: "Hebrews claims that God spoke to our fathers, in the past, through the prophets. Hebrews also claims that God has spoken to us, in the last of days, through a son. In Hebrews, Jesus is a living word, and in the preaching experience, He is alive today."[5]

---

[5] Luke Johnson, "The World Imagined by Scripture."

I

Part 1:

Essays on Preaching Hebrews

1

Hebrews' Challenge to Christians:

Christology and Discipleship

Luke Timothy Johnson

The Letter to the Hebrews is one of the few theological masterpieces in the New Testament canon. For depth of perception and strength of argumentation, it finds a match only in Paul; for power of imagination and breadth of vision, only John's Gospel is its equal. Hebrews may owe its place in the New Testament canon, indeed, to the impressive character of its thought and expression. Lacking the sponsorship of any definite author or location—although it traveled for a time as part of the Pauline corpus—Hebrews was nevertheless quickly and unanimously regarded as an "apostolic" voice. It is thoroughly appropriated by Clement in his letter to the Corinthian church (ca. 95), and is vigorously exploited by patristic interpreters, who found in Hebrews a critical resource especially for thinking through Trinitarian and Christological issues.

Hebrews does not enjoy equivalent favor among contemporary Christians. Some reasons are obvious. Hebrews makes its impact by means of a single sustained argument and does not yield easily divided and digestible portions for edification of readers. Hebrews carries out its argument by means of frequent and lengthy biblical citations and allusions rather than by responding to specific problems among the readers. Readers of today, who can think their way into First Corinthians because the issues in that church resemble those found among all communities, find little in Hebrews with which they can identify. And with the decline in biblical literacy, the full impact—or even the point—of Hebrews' careful scriptural argument is not easily available. Finally, Hebrews is manifestly alien to the world of contemporary readers, especially in its Platonic world-view, and in its attention to the sacrificial cult. People today don't have much philosophy generally, but if they have some, it is certainly not a form of Platonism. What Hebrews assumes to be true about reality—that the spiritual is superior to the material, for example—is by no means self-evident to present-day readers. As for the language of sacrifice, a long tradition of anti-sacrificial rhetoric among Christians, sharpened today by perceptions that "self-sacrifice" is bad for women and other oppressed peoples, makes Hebrews' symbolism of choice less than attractive. This "otherness" is certainly present in other New Testament writings as well. When Paul casually mentions baptizing people for the dead, or the need to veil women's heads because of the angels, he refers to things and ideas not in the repertoire of present-day readers. But constant reading of Paul, like the constant reinterpretation of the Gospels, tends to soften the material's alien character, so that contemporary readers can imagine themselves living in the same world. Hebrews is so clearly and defiantly alien that it resists our easy assimilation.

These are the very reasons, in contrast, that make Hebrews a favorite New Testament composition among scholars. Precisely the ways in which Hebrews is different make it fascinating and worth studying. Such scholarship is concerned, however, not with living within the world constructed by Hebrews, but only with understanding the world that produced Hebrews. The letter is interpreted by being explained in terms of the world out of which it emerged. Thus, the Platonism that is so remote from ordinary readers is familiar to the student of antiquity, who can trace the ways in which Hebrews both continues and deviates from the patterns of Greek thought. Christians who simply want to know what Hebrews meant are magnificently assisted by an abundance of genuinely fine scholarship devoted to disentangling such issues. But what of the Christian who asks what the world of Hebrews has to do with Christians today? Is its world one so removed from our own that all we can do is explain it as an interesting artifact from the past? Does Hebrews make any present claim on us as Christians?

The real test case is Hebrews' understanding of Christ and of Christian discipleship. These are the subjects, after all, to which all Hebrews' scriptural interpretation, Platonic world-view, use of sacrificial imagery, and rhetorical argument, are dedicated. Is the Jesus of Hebrews also alien? Is its understanding of Christian discipleship removed from our own? These are the issues that should concern us, for no amount of explaining will help, when it comes to the center of our existence and the pattern of our lives as Christians. In this essay, I argue that although the Christology of Hebrews and its understanding of discipleship may seem strange in some ways to contemporary readers, this is as much because of the condition of Christology and discipleship today as it is because of Hebrews. In fact, I propose that one of the most valuable contributions Hebrews can make today is to challenge present-day convictions and practices on these two deeply interrelated topics.

Christology in Hebrews

We can approach the Christology of Hebrews by noting its unusually rich display of titles for Jesus. Some of them are common in the earliest Christian literature. The letter uses the simple name "Jesus" frequently, corresponding to its interest in his humanity (2:9; 3:1; 4:14; 6:20; 7:22; 10:19; 12:24; 13:12, 20). Almost as frequently it uses the title "Christ" (3:6, 14; 5:5; 6:1; 9:11, 14, 24, 28). The combination "Jesus Christ" occurs only three times (10:10; 13:8, 21). Hebrews speaks often of the Son (1:2, 5, 8; 3:6; 5:5, 8; 7:28) as well as "Son of God" (4:14; 6:6; 7:3; 10:29) and "Lord" (1:10; 2:3; 7:14; 13:20). By implication, Hebrews ascribes the designation "Son of Man" to Jesus (2:6; see Psalm 8:4), and its use of Psalm 45:6-7 in 1:8 implies that Jesus is properly designated by the title "God" (*theos*). Other titles for Jesus are either unique in the New Testament or are rare. Jesus is referred to as "heir" (1:2), "the first-born" (1:6), "the great shepherd of the sheep" (13:20), "the pioneer" (2:10; 12:2), and the "perfector" (12:2). He is the "sanctifier" (2:11), the "apostle" (3:1), and the "builder of God's house" (3:3). He is the "cause of salvation" (5:9), the "forerunner" (6:20), the "guarantor" (7:22), the "minister"

(8:2), and the "mediator" (8:6; 9:15; 12:24). These special titles can be viewed synoptically to reveal the two main emphases of Christology in Hebrews. Jesus is the one who brings salvation from God to humanity (apostle, cause, sanctifier, shepherd, minister, builder, guarantor). He is also a human being who reaches first what all seek (heir, first-born, pioneer, forerunner, perfector). As the one who accomplishes both, he is supremely the mediator.

These two aspects come together in the titles that Hebrews alone ascribes to Jesus, drawn from the language of Jewish sacrificial cult. Hebrews is not alone in picturing Jesus' death and resurrection in terms of sacrifice. Paul says that "Christ our Pasch (lamb) has been sacrificed" (1 Cor 5:7) and speaks of Jesus' death in terms of the sprinkling of blood on the mercy-seat on the day of atonement (Rom 3:25). Peter speaks of the precious blood of Christ that is like that of a lamb (1 Pet 1:21). John says that the blood of Jesus cleanses us all from sin (1 John 1:7), and Revelation portrays Jesus as the Lamb who was slain (Rev 5:12). The Synoptic accounts of Jesus' last meal with his disciples, furthermore, speak of the cup as the blood of the covenant poured out for many (Matt 26:27). Hebrews is alone, however, in explicitly designating Jesus as a priest (10:21), high priest (3:1; 4:14; 5:5, 10; 6:20; 7:26; 8:1; 9:11), and a "merciful and faithful High Priest" (2:17). The priestly title is throughout the letter associated with royal imagery, drawn from the combination of terms in Ps 110:1-4. Jesus is priest as the Lord who has taken his seat at the right hand of God. He is priest-king (see 1:3, 8, 13; 2:5, 7, 9; 4:16; 7:1, 2; 8:1; 10:12; 12:2, 28).

This array of titles for Jesus reveals how Hebrews escapes the easy categorizations so often applied to Christology. Here, the contrast between high and low Christology (or "Christology from above" and "Christology from below") is as inapplicable as that between "early" and "late" or between "simple" and "complex." Hebrews is possibly among our earliest Christian writings. Yet, as in Paul, we see an astonishingly complex apprehension of the figure of Jesus, one that emphasizes at the same time his divine status and his human work. Indeed, that bifocal perception of Jesus is critical to the argument concerning him and his work that Hebrews seeks to make. I do not suggest that Chalcedon can be read off the pages of Hebrews, but I do suggest that Chalcedon can be found in the pages of Hebrews. As uncomfortable with metaphysics as some of us are these days, it nevertheless makes sense to appreciate the ontological dimensions of Hebrews' language concerning Jesus.

On one side, then, Hebrews emphasizes that Jesus Christ is divine. The point is made most emphatically by the letter's opening words. God spoke in partial and multiple ways to the ancestors in the past through the prophets, but now speaks through a Son (1:1-2). The author immediately makes clear in 1:1-3 that "Son of God" here means much more than the sort of metaphor that was routinely applied to the kings of antiquity. This Son is the heir of all things, is the one through whom God created the world, and upholds the universe by his word of power. These three expressions place the Son at the origin of all things with God, sustaining all things, and at the end, receiving all things. Between these "functional" statements, the author applies to the Son two characterizations that echo the Book of Wisdom 7:25-26, and that can only be taken as statements about "being": "He is the reflection of God's glory and the imprint of God's very being." It is noteworthy that in these opening statements, Hebrews makes no real distinction between the various stages of Christ's existence. The statements concerning his "being" seem to apply whether we think of his role in creation, or his making purification for sins, or his taking his place at the right hand of the majesty on high (1:1-3).

The stress on the divine character of Christ is scarcely confined to the prologue. Creation is once more directly attributed to him in 1:10 through the citation of Psalm 102:25-27: "Thou, Lord, didst found the earth in the beginning and the heavens are the work of your hands." The world that he created is also subject to him (2:5-8). That the Son is greater than the angels is the burden of all the citations in 1:5-14; unlike the angels, he is to be worshipped (1:6). And who can be worshipped but God? The title *theos* is ordinarily reserved for the Father in the New Testament. Every application to Christ either carries an etiolated sense or is disputed (see John 1:1, 18; Rom 9:5; Tit 2:13). But the designation appears to be intended to be taken with full weight in 1:8, where Psalm 45:6-7 is applied to Jesus: "When he brings the first-born into the world, he says, 'Your throne O God is forever and ever, and the righteous scepter is the scepter of your kingdom." The fact that the Psalm citation continues, "You have loved righteousness and hated wickedness; therefore God your God has anointed you," (1:9) does not seem to bother the author at all. Indeed, the same tension is found in John 1:18, where the "only begotten God" (according to the best manuscripts) reveals the God "whom no one has ever seen." Out of such stretching of language to express the mystery of what was experienced in Jesus Christ arose the need for the more precise diction of philosophy that eventually found its permanent home in the Nicene-Constantinopolitan Creed.

When Hebrews calls Jesus "Son," therefore, it means this in the fullest possible sense: Jesus is and does what God is and does. It is because he is divine that he can be "cause of eternal salvation" to those who believe in him (5:9), and can come again "to save those who are eagerly waiting for him" (9:28). Although he was made "for a little while lower than the angels," he has been crowned with glory and honor (2:9), and "he is able for all time to save those who draw near to God through him, since he always lives to make intercession for them" (7:25). This last passage continues, "It was fitting that we should have such a high priest, holy, blameless, unstained, separated from sinners, exalted above the heavens...the word of oath, which came later than the law, appoints a Son who has been made perfect forever... we have such a high priest, one who is seated at the right hand of the throne of God" (7:26-8:1).

Just as emphatically, Hebrews insists on the full humanity of the Son. The one made "lower than the angels" is the "Son of Man" of Psalm 8:4, to whom God subjects the world to come (Heb 2:1-8). The common nature of Jesus and "his brothers" is elaborated in 2:10-18, which rhetorically answers the emphasis on his divinity in chapter one. The one who sanctifies (Christ) and the ones who are sanctified, Hebrews declares, "are all from one," meaning that they share the same ancestry or origin, and therefore have a common identity (2:10). It is appropriate therefore, to follow Scripture in calling humans his "brothers" and also "his children" (2:12-13), since these children share flesh and blood and "he himself shares in them as well" (2:14). Like all other humans, Christ tastes death (2:14). And like all humans, he belongs to a very specific human lineage: he belongs to the family of Abraham (2:16). He is like his brothers in every respect (*kata panta homoiothenai*, 2:17), including the experiencing of temptation (or testing, *peirazein*, 2:18). This last quality is repeated and qualified in 4:15, which says of Jesus that he was "tested as we are yet without sin." Because Jesus shares so fully in the common condition of humanity, he is able to experience the emotions humans feel with regard to their fellows. He can be a "merciful and faithful" high priest because he has experienced the trials that others have (2:17-18). He can "deal gently with those who are ignorant and erring since he himself is beset by weakness" (5:2).

These human characteristics are all on display in Hebrews' description of Jesus "in the days of his flesh," making prayers and petitions to God. He prayed with "loud cries and tears" and he was heard because of his pious submission to God (5:7). I will return to the remainder of this remarkable passage shortly. But for now, we can note the steady emphasis on Jesus' full humanity. It is not certain that the author of Hebrews had in mind a specific incident of Jesus' life, although the resemblance to Jesus' prayer before his death has frequently been noted (see Matt 26:38-46//; John 12:27). Are we to read into this short description the additional nuance that Jesus not only experienced death but also the "terror of death" by which all humans are held captive (2:15)? We cannot be sure. But that Jesus had to approach God in the same way as other humans, that he expressed profound and negative human feelings through "loud cries and tears," and that he had the human religious disposition of pious submission (*eulabeia*), all of this is clear enough. Also clear and striking is the allusion to the manner of Jesus' human death, which was the most shameful imaginable in the Greco-Roman world, crucifixion (6:6). He "suffered outside the gate" and bore "his reviling outside the camp" (13:12-13). But he "despised the shame of the cross" because of the joy that was set before him (12:2).

Hebrews develops its portrayal of Jesus as High Priest

precisely on the basis of this gritty and shameful human experience. Unlike other priests, as we have seen, Jesus is God's own Son. But like other priests, he is "taken from among humans for the sake of humans" (5:1). In its dramatic appropriation (and adaptation) of LXX Psalm 39:7-9 in 10:5-8, Hebrews makes clear that it is Christ's body and will that are the instruments of his priestly activity. The Psalm is made to say, "sacrifices and offerings you have not desired, but a body (*soma*) you have prepared for me," which replaces the "ears" (*ota*) of the Septuagint passage being quoted. The citation from the Psalm concludes with "See I have come (in the scroll of the book it is written concerning me) to do your will, O God" (10:7). This willingness of Jesus to do God's will is singled out by Hebrews as the effective replacement of the sacrifices of old that God no longer seeks (10:9), and it concludes, "it is by that will that we have been sanctified by the offering once for all of the body of Jesus Christ" (10:10). Jesus has entered into the true holy place, which is the presence of the eternal God, with his own blood (9:12-14), which he offered for the sins of many (9:28). His flesh is the curtain through which he has entered into God's presence, thereby opening up a "new and more perfect way" of access to God for other humans (10:19). He is therefore the forerunner (6:20), the pioneer who goes ahead of others (12:2). And he is so because he is the one who is the finisher or perfector of faith (12:2). This last aspect of Jesus' humanity draws us into the deepest dimension of the Christology of Hebrews, and the dimension most difficult to explore, which is the role of Christ's suffering.

This theme is announced in 2:10, "It was fitting that He, for whom and by whom all things exist, in bringing many sons to glory, should make the pioneer of their salvation perfect through suffering." There are four discrete aspects of the statement worth isolating. First, we notice how Jesus is to be first among others. He is the pioneer among "many sons" whom God is bringing to glory. We can infer, then, that what happens to him is available also to his brothers. Second, Jesus as human undergoes a process of perfection. It is when he has "been made perfect" (*teleiotheis*, 5:9) that he can be a cause of salvation to those who obey him.

The cognates of *teleioun* ("to bring to perfection") run throughout Hebrews. The term has obvious religious and moral associations in antiquity. One who is *teleios* has finished a course of initiations, is more mature, is further along, is better, than one who is not. The notions of comparison and of progress are ingredients to such language. Thus, the tent in which Jesus offers himself is "more perfect" than that in the wilderness (9:11), and the Levitical priesthood could not bring "perfection" to worshippers (7:11; 9:9; 10:1), just as the Law could "perfect" no one (7:19). In contrast, the sacrifice of Jesus has brought to perfection those it sanctifies forever (10:14). Those who had faith in earlier generations were not perfected apart from the present generation (11:40), but the readers of Hebrews approach the place where reside the spirits of the righteous who have been brought to perfection (12:23). These readers must turn from milk to the solid food that is appropriate to the perfect (mature, 5:14) and the author's discourse will lead them toward such considerations of perfection (6:1).

Third, we see that suffering is the means by which Jesus reaches the perfection that enables him to save his brethren (2:10). Finally, Hebrews declares as appropriate this path toward perfection which Jesus has pioneered and which others are to follow ("it is fitting," 2:10). In order to understand this appropriateness, we must consider first what Hebrews might mean by "suffering," and then how it can play a role in moral transformation.

Hebrews itself points the way to this consideration by the second passage in which "perfection" and "suffering" occur together. We have already looked at 5:7-9 as a passage in which the humanity of Jesus was expressed with particular vividness. But we did not observe the key clause in 5:8-9: "although he was a Son, he learned obedience from the things he suffered, and having been perfected, he became the cause of salvation to all those who obey him." What is suffering? And what suffering is being referred to here?

We can begin by defining suffering as the pain consequent to the disequilibrium of a sentient system. This neutral definition enables us to see that only sentient beings can suffer but also that they can suffer in a number of ways and with both negative and positive valence. Sentient systems can be physical, mental, emotional, or spiritual. So long as a system is in equilibrium, it does not experience pain. But pain is an inevitable consequence of disequilibrium. A body experiences pain through injury or disease. But it also experiences pain through growth or muscular exertion or childbirth. Pain is neither good nor bad in itself. It is simply a signal concerning the system. Similarly, emotional pain can result both from fear and intense desire. Likewise, mental pain inevitably follows upon the enlargement of one's mental universe. Indeed, the perception that the education of the body, mind, and emotions required pain (suffering) was one of the great insights of ancient philosophy, typically distilled in a maxim, *mathein pathein*, "to learn is to suffer," which can of course also be converted to, "to suffer is to learn."

Contemporaries who think of this in terms of physical training for athletics would perhaps translate idiomatically as "no pain, no gain," and capture the idea perfectly. The training of the body and spirit went together in ancient culture, which used the same term, *paideia*, for both "culture" and "education." Notice that in this conception, suffering is not the result of something inflicted from the outside, but is rather intrinsic to certain processes of growth or maturation. In the case of Jesus, the passage in Hebrews 5:7-9 does not refer explicitly to the suffering that Jesus' body experienced in his passion but to a process of suffering that he experienced before his actual death. The author connects it to his prayers and petitions with loud cries and tears in the days of his flesh (5:7). The suffering is ingredient to Jesus' response of faith and trust in God, his *eulabeia* (5:7). Hebrews identifies this as "obedience" (*hypakoe*) in 5:8, "He learned obedience from the things he suffered," and connects his "being made perfect" directly to this process (5:9). Jesus' suffering, therefore, was part of a process through which he learned how to be Son; his obedience to God was the way in which he became more fully that which he was, God's Son. This process was brought to its completion in his death and exaltation.

If we have understood these passages correctly, then the Christology of Hebrews is far from a static or mechanical juxtaposition of "two natures in one person." Rather, the letter suggests that the human Jesus progressively grew into his stature of divine Son. Through his human faith and obedience, he progressively opened himself to the mystery of God. Such opening to mystery inevitably involves pain or suffering, just as pain and suffering have the capacity of opening humans to the mystery of God. Leon Bloy says somewhere that there are places in the heart that do not yet exist but only come into being through suffering. In the heart of the human being Jesus, God increasingly took occupation, carved an ever-greater space for God's own freedom. Or, to put it another way, the divine within him progressively found more explicit expression in the freedom of the human person Jesus. Viewed in this fashion, the moment of death, which appears from the outside to be the final and ultimate closure, the shutting down of existence, became for Jesus the ultimate opening of his humanity to the presence of God. In that moment, he "stepped through the veil of his flesh" and in his death and exaltation opened a new and better way of access to God: not a way established externally through the sacrifice of animals, but internally through the body and freedom of human response. He is the pioneer of faith because he went first. He is the perfector of faith because he himself was perfected through it.

Discipleship in Hebrews

Hebrews calls itself a "word of exhortation" (*logos tes parakleseos*, 13:22), and the main goal of its rhetoric is transparent. It seeks to maintain and even strengthen the loyalty of believers against the temptation to fall away in the face of difficulties (2:1-3; 4:1-2, 11-16; 6:4-12; 10:19-39; 12:1-28). Thus, the importance of its Christological argument: showing that Christ, as the Son through whom God has definitively spoken, is the bearer of a greater hope and the High Priest of a better covenant, provides the motivation for such loyalty. If the promise of life through Christ is greater, so also is the threat of punishment for those who abandon this promise (see 10:19-31). The roll call of witnesses in Hebrews 11 serves to support this exhortation to fidelity. The author reminds his readers that the ancient witnesses—like them (10:32-35)—also suffered loss of land and family, experienced hardships, wandered as aliens and strangers, seeking a "city with foundations" (11:8-16), yet they remained loyal to the God who called them. They did not sell their birthright for a pot of porridge (12:16). So also, Hebrews says, "we are not of those who shrink back and are destroyed, but of those who have faith and keep their souls" (10:39).

Added to this central exhortation, Hebrews, in chapter 13, encourages its readers to the common virtues of the Christian life: brotherly love (13:1; see 6:10), hospitality (13:2), visiting those in prison (13:3; see 10:34), avoiding sexual immorality and keeping marriage holy (13:4), avoiding love of money and cultivating contentment (13:5-6; see 10:34), avoiding strange teachings (13:9), imitating the faith of their leaders (13:7) and obeying them gladly (13:17), sharing their possessions (13:16), and praying (13:15; 18-19). Each of these instructions can easily be matched many times by other New Testament writings. But Hebrews adds two statements in chapter thirteen that catch our eye because of their distinctiveness. They invite us to look more closely at its understanding of discipleship. Does it mean something more than holding on to the confession and practicing virtue?

The first statement is the conclusion of the prayer in 13:20-21. The God of peace is asked "to equip you with everything good that you may do his will, working in you that which is pleasing in his sight, through Jesus Christ" (13: 21). Just as it was Jesus' obedience to God's will that caused their salvation (10:10), so are they to do the will of God. But notice that they do this by "God working in (or among) them." And notice further that his working and their doing is *dia Iesou Christou*, "through Jesus Christ." Read in this fashion, the prayer closely connects Jesus' obedience toward God and theirs, so much so that it appears that it is "through Jesus," that God works their obedience. The second statement is the observation and exhortation in 13:12-13: "So Jesus also suffered outside the gate in order to sanctify the people through his own blood. Therefore let us go forth to him outside the camp and bear the abuse he endured." Here we find the closest possible connection between the example of the human Jesus and the behavior of his followers. They are to embrace the suffering he endured as their own.

These statements in chapter 13 suggest that we understand Jesus as "pioneer and perfector of faith" in the sense that what God worked in him is meant to be worked in his followers as well. Jesus is not only the Son of God who is the cause of salvation. He is also our forerunner who shows us in his own faith the pattern of our own. That Hebrews intends just this sort of understanding is supported by the elaborate athletic imagery of chapter 12. The author masterfully evokes the scene of an athletic contest, specifically a race. There is the "cloud of witnesses" cheering on the contestants (12:1). Jesus is the pacesetter and first finisher (12:2). The readers, in turn, are urged to "run with perseverance the [same] race that is set before [them]." They are to throw off whatever weighs them down, just as athletes are to strip themselves for action (12:1). They are to avoid the easy distractions of sin (12:1). They are to "look to Jesus" and "consider Jesus" running ahead of them (12:2, 3; see 3:1).

The athletic terminology continues in 12:11, where it is noted that all "discipline" (*paideia*) seems painful rather than pleasant, but that it later yields good results for those "who have been trained in it" (*gegymnasmenos*). Compare 5:14, where the writer states that solid food is for the "mature, for those who have their faculties trained by practice" (*dia ten hexin ta aistheteria gegymnasmena*). Hebrews 12:12 continues the athletic imagery: "Therefore lift your drooping hands and strengthen your weak knees and make straight paths for your feet, so that what is lame may not be put out of joint but rather healed." This set of exhortations fits those running a race!

I have emphasized this athletic language in order to make sense of Hebrews 12:5-11. At first sight, it is one of the most puzzling passages in the letter, an apparently extraneous excursus. But properly understood, it offers the real point of the author's teaching on discipleship. The passage clearly refers to the afflictions the community has been experiencing (see 10:32-35), which, the author says, have not yet reached the point of their shedding their blood (12:4). How should they view the hard things happening to them? They should regard them as the discipline (*paideia*) imposed by a father on a beloved son (12:5-6, citing LXX Proverbs 3:11-12). Fathers only discipline the sons they acknowledge as their own, says the author; they fail to discipline their bastard children (12:7-8). The logic here may disturb present-day readers who think in terms of the physical abuse of children "because we love you." It is therefore necessary to place ourselves imaginatively in ancient patriarchal cultures. The issue is not physical abuse, but training in character, as 12:10-11 makes clear. Ancient moralists like Xenophon and Plutarch were well aware how refractory human nature could be, and how much discipline was required to form good habits. They understood that moral education was a matter of transformation of mind and attitude as well as of body, and that this transformation involved painful change.

In this context, we notice two important aspects of 12:5-ll. The first is that the language of father and son is scarcely accidental. Jesus is God's Son preeminently, but being perfected through what he suffered, he is to lead "many sons to glory" (2:10). Hebrews places the suffering of the community within the framework of the suffering of Jesus as God's Son. They are experiencing what he did. This is why they are told, "consider him who endured from sinners such hostility against himself, so that you may not grow weary or fainthearted" (12:3). The second thing we notice is that this passage also picks up the theme of education through suffering announced in 5:8 (although he was a Son, he learned obedience through what he suffered). We remember that the term here translated as "discipline" (*paideia*) was used broadly in Greco-Roman culture to mean both culture and education. The suffering now experienced by the readers is to be their education in obedience as "sons" just as Jesus as God's Son learned obedience from what he suffered (*emathen aph' hon epathen*). Thus, the best translation of the short sentence in 12:7, *eis paideian hypomenete,* is probably not the RSV's "It is for discipline that you have to endure," or even the NRSV's "Endure trials for the sake of discipline." Or the NAB's "Endure your trials as discipline." All these translations take the verb as an imperative and miss the double sense of *paideia*. It is better to take the verb as an indicative and to translate, "you are enduring for the sake of an education." And why they should endure is made clear by the next verse: "God is treating you as sons!"

The meaning of discipleship in Hebrews is not merely a matter of loyalty to the profession of Christian or the doing of virtue. It means living like all the heroes of faith who lived as strangers and aliens on the earth, seeking God's city: "Here we have no lasting city, but we seek a city which is to come" (13:14). It means following in the path of the suffering Jesus, and being transformed through God's power, as he was, into genuine children of God through the obedience of faith that progressively opens us to God's fearful freedom. It means enduring for the sake of an education (12:7). It means "going forth to him outside the camp and bearing the abuse he endured' (13:13).

The Challenge of Hebrews

Christian readers today ought to be challenged by Hebrews, not because its language is daunting or its symbolism is alien, but because its understanding of Jesus Christ and of discipleship is at odds with that held by many who consider themselves Christian.

The rich and complex apprehension of Jesus that we find in Hebrews is today split asunder. Perhaps because of the contemporary distaste for ontology and the flat epistemological monism that has characterized modernity, it appears impossible for many to hold together the divine and human poles in the person of Jesus. On one side we find the fervent profession of Jesus as Son of God. Those who emphasize the divinity of Christ, however, sometimes slight the full significance of his humanity. The human Jesus tends to be swallowed up by the Trinity. Jesus is the object of faith and of prayer. His help is sought in every matter. But there is little sense of how Jesus is exemplar of life. The slogan "what would Jesus do" remains external and superficial. But for all its deficiencies, this overemphasis at least maintains continuity with the doctrinal convictions of the church through the ages, and at least comports with the logic of Christian piety.

The other Christological extreme is represented by the quest for the historical Jesus. Here, the humanity of Jesus is so emphasized that any consideration of his divine nature is taken as a doctrinal imposition that must be sheared away if the "real Jesus" is to be discovered through the process of historical reconstruction. The positive effect of this effort has been to recover some of the sense of Jesus' rootedness in the world of the first century and in particular his Jewishness, but the costs have been high. Quite apart from the distortions of historical method required to carry out such reconstructions, and the mutually exclusive portraits of the human Jesus that result—usually a mirror-image of the investigators—the "human Jesus" ends up as a sociological stereotype rather than the robust character portrayed by the Gospels and the writings of the New Testament as a whole. Some insight may have been gained into Jesus' Jewish identity and the social or political implications of his activity, but an appreciation for his human character and for the religious implications of his presence have been lost. As simply another human figure of the past, Jesus appears as one who at most rearranged the structures of society, rather than—as Christian faith has always proclaimed—one whose life, death, and resurrection have fundamentally altered the structures of human existence itself.

Against this disjunctive and distorted set of Christologies, Hebrews demands taking Jesus both as fully God and as fully human, as essential to the adequate apprehension of who Jesus is. Hebrews asserts as strongly as the Gospel of John the divine character of Jesus, and it asserts as forcefully as Luke his humanity. Hebrews is not capable of showing how this paradox can be maintained. But it provides a hint when it speaks of the manner in which Jesus became perfected as Son through his suffering. It allows us to imagine, not a grotesque hybrid, but rather a human person who was more and more human as he was opened more and more to the divine, and a son of God who was perfected in his Sonship precisely through his humanity.

There is a similar disjunction among present-day Christians concerning discipleship, corresponding to the two distorted Christologies. On one side, there is the peculiar phenomenon of the "Gospel of Success," in which the profession of Jesus as Lord, a personal relationship with him in faith, and a reliance upon his divine assistance in every circumstance will lead to a life free from stress and suffering, one overflowing in material prosperity and human happiness. Discipleship is here equated with right belief and right practice, spelled out in the consistent moral teachings of the church through the ages, each understood in highly individualistic fashion. If Christians engage the social or political order, it is precisely to secure the social dominance of these codes and the political security in which to practice them. In this understanding of discipleship, physical or mental or emotional suffering is a sign of failed faith.

Corresponding to the Christology that focuses on the humanity of Jesus is a vision of discipleship that is completely ordered to the transformation of social and political structures. Being a follower of the prophet Jesus means living out a vision of the social gospel that is liberating for those who are marginalized and oppressed. The social order must be precisely rearranged, for sin is understood as social rather than personal in character. Racism, sexism, age-ism, capitalism, and species-ism are systems that are intrinsically distortive of true human dignity and must be changed if the good news is to be realized. Once more, amazingly, suffering is excluded from discipleship. The suffering of the oppressed and marginalized has no value for them or anyone else. It must be eliminated. Its continuance in the world is a witness to failed discipleship. One might, it is true, suffer in the trenches in the battle against the powers and principalities. But one is freed from the mental and emotional suffering that is inherent in ambiguity because, like those who dwell securely within the alternative view of discipleship, this sentient system is totally in equilibrium, since it is totally certain of being right.

The Letter to the Hebrews challenges both these distorted forms of discipleship. On one side, it calls for utter loyalty to the profession of faith and the keeping of the most traditional forms of moral rectitude. But on the other side, it calls for hospitality toward strangers, for some have unwittingly played host to angels! It calls for brotherly love. It calls for sharing possessions. It demands the visiting of prisoners and those who are ill treated, "since you also are in the body" (13:3). In a word, the intense piety of Hebrews is not individualistic but communal, not a seeking of the self (even the self's salvation) but a care for the community. And most of all, Hebrews makes suffering the very heart of discipleship. Suffering is not merely a matter of things that happen to people from the outside, although it is clear that Hebrews could not conceive of a Christianity that considered the loss of property and imprisonment as judgments on an inadequate faith! Suffering, rather, is ingredient to the obedience of faith itself. It is an inevitable concomitant of opening oneself to the presence and the power of God. It is the essential means by which humans become transformed into God's true and beloved children.

2

From Narrative Text to Discursive Sermon:
The Challenge of Hebrews
Charles L. Campbell

The form of the text should shape the form of the sermon. This little axiom has become an important presupposition of contemporary, mainline homiletics. Poetic texts should be preached poetically. Parables should be preached parabolically. Narratives should be preached narratively. Admittedly, we don't hear much about deductive texts being preached deductively or theological arguments being preached argumentatively. Some genres are more popular than others these days. But the basic presupposition generally holds: the form of the text should shape the form of the sermon.

This presupposition has made an important contribution to contemporary homiletics. Because of it, there has been an explosion of new sermon forms in recent years. No longer do preachers simply try to force a text into a single, artificial mold. Rather, variety rules the day, and that has been a healthy development for both preachers and congregations.

In particular, this presupposition has played an important role in the development of narrative preaching. Narrative sermons are necessary, the argument goes, because much of Scripture takes the form of story. H. Grady Davis, in his seminal book, *Design for Preaching*, which turned the attention of contemporary homiletics to sermon form, stated this argument clearly:

> ...we preachers forget that the gospel itself is for the most part a simple narrative of persons, places,

happenings, and conversation. It is not a verbal
exposition of general ideas. Nine-tenths of our
preaching is verbal exposition and argument, but not
one tenth of the gospel is exposition. Its ideas are
mainly in the form of a story told.[1]

Thus were the seeds for narrative preaching planted in
the ground of the narrative shape of Scripture. Although other
arguments have been made for the turn to story in contemporary
homiletics, the assumption that the form of the sermon should
be shaped by the form of the text has played a significant role.

Unfortunately, Hebrews wreaks havoc with this assumption.
Commonly recognized as one of the best examples of an early
Christian sermon, Hebrews represents a largely discursive (non-
narrative) sermon that is based on a narrative text—the story of
Jesus. Hebrews thus confronts the contemporary preacher with a
dilemma. If the preacher preaches a sermon on Hebrews shaped
by the form of Hebrews itself (as contemporary homileticians
suggest), the preacher will actually have to preach a discursive
sermon—a theological argument—based on a narrative text
(something contemporary homileticians discourage). Hebrews,
that is, challenges a simplistic move from the form of the text to
the form of the sermon; it suggests that the relationship between
the biblical text and its homiletical appropriation is complex, not
only hermeneutically but also formally. In what follows, I will
examine the relationship between narrative text and discursive
speech in Hebrews and then explore some of the homiletical
implications for us today.

Like most preachers, the preacher of Hebrews begins by
setting forth the text for the sermon:

Long ago God spoke to our ancestors in many and
various ways by the prophets, but in these last days
God has spoken to us by a Son whom God appointed
heir of all things, through whom God also created the
worlds. He is the reflection of God's glory and the
exact imprint of God's very being, and he sustains

---

[1]H. Grady Davis, *Design for Preaching* (Philadelphia: Fortress, 1958), 157.

all things by his powerful word. When he had made purification for sins, he sat down at the right hand of the Majesty on high, having become as much superior to angels as the name he has inherited is more excellent than theirs. (1:1-4)

Rather than using a specific text from the Hebrew Scriptures, the preacher's text is a particular—and grand—story of Jesus, most of the components of which are highlighted in these opening four verses:

- Jesus existed before creation, and through him all things were created;
- for a little while he was made lower than angels (implying the incarnation, including the assertion that, as a human being, he is the reflection of God's glory and the imprint of God's very being; not surprisingly this text appears during Christmas in the Revised Common Lectionary);
- he made purification for sins (a reference to his death and its purpose);
- he sat down at the right hand of the Majesty on high (which implies both his resurrection and his ascension);
- he is the heir of all things—the one to whom all things come.[2]

This story of Jesus is the text for the entire sermon. It provides the starting point and the recurring "theme" for the sermon. As in a piece of jazz, the preacher of Hebrews states this theme at the beginning and then returns to it repeatedly throughout the sermon, sometimes in a rather complete form, at other times through more partial or subtle allusions. Along the way, between statements of this narrative theme, the preacher

---

[2] Often referred to as the "prologue" to Hebrews, verses 1-4 provide the basic text that will shape the entire sermon. The central role this story plays in the sermon will become clear in what follows. Hebrews 9:28 adds another component to this story: he will "appear a second time" in order "to save those who are eagerly waiting for him."

interprets this story in discursive form, providing new insights into the story.

A couple of examples indicate the central role this story plays in Hebrews. In 2:9, for example, where the preacher stresses the importance of "seeing Jesus," central components of the story are recounted.

> As it is, we do not see everything in subjection to [human beings], but we do see Jesus, who for a little while was made lower than the angels, now crowned with glory and honor because of the suffering of death, so that by the grace of God he might taste death for everyone.

Similarly, but in much more complex fashion, the preacher in Chapter 7 relates the same basic story, this time through the figure of Jesus as a high priest after the order of Melchizedek. At the beginning of the most extended theological argument in the sermon, the preacher once again highlights the central elements of the story. Of Melchizedek (and alluding to Jesus), the preacher notes: He is "without mother, father, genealogy, having neither beginning of days nor end of life—resembling the Son of God" (7:3; compare 1:2). A clear allusion to Jesus' resurrection occurs in 7:8, when the preacher again says of Melchizedek that he is "one of whom it is testified that he lives." Beginning in 7:11, the preacher speaks directly of Jesus; and once again the central components of the story come to the fore: he became a priest through the power of an indestructible life (7:16; resurrection); he was exalted above the heavens (7:26; ascension); he offered sacrifice once and for all when he offered himself (7:27; crucifixion, with humanity implicit); he was "made perfect forever" (7:28; resurrection); he is the high priest, "seated at the right hand of the throne of Majesty" (8:1; ascension).[3] In this critical section of the letter, the preacher of Hebrews repeatedly alludes to the central narrative that shapes the entire sermon.

---

[3] For other places where the preacher of Hebrews returns to this story see, for example 9:23-28; 10:12; 12:1-3; 13:12; 13:20. Throughout the letter, ongoing allusions to this story appear.

Several points can be made about the centrality of this story in Hebrews. First, the centrality and regular recurrence of this story highlights the Christocentric focus of Hebrews, with which few would argue. The preacher fundamentally seeks to help the congregation see, understand, trust, and follow Jesus. The story that shapes the sermon is the story of Jesus.

Second, consistent with the Christocentric focus of the sermon, "story" functions primarily to render the identity of Jesus. Although applied specifically to Jesus, this use of narrative is a common one; when we wish to render the identity of a person in his or her richness and complexity, we turn to story. That is the primary reason the gospels are narrative in form; in order to render the complexity of Jesus' identity, the gospel writers must tell his story. The preacher of Hebrews uses narrative in a similar way. The preacher, that is, shows no interest in the genre of narrative per se, but turns to story primarily to identify Jesus, who is the focus of the sermon. In other words, narrative serves the identity of Jesus. All of the interpretive work in Hebrews flows from the basic narrative that renders Jesus' identity—his person and work. The preacher returns to this narrative again and again throughout the sermon as a reminder that no single interpretation can capture the richness and complexity of the story itself. Discursive argument may expound on Jesus' identity, but it inevitably captures only one angle of the story and limits its richness. Story remains essential for rendering Jesus' identity and consequently plays a central role in Hebrews.

Third, the story of Jesus is linked to the larger story of Israel through figural or typological interpretation. In 1:1-4, the preacher affirms that the new, last-days speech of God through a Son is linked to the larger story of Israel in the word of the prophets. Something radically new has arrived (so new that Hebrews has supercessionist tendencies), but that new thing will be interpreted figurally through the persons, institutions, and events in the story of Israel. In chapter 7, which, as I noted above, retells the story of Jesus through the figure of the high priest after the order of Melchizedek, the linking of the story of Jesus with the story of Israel through figural interpretation is developed most fully.

Story thus plays a critical, foundational role in Hebrews. Having noted this fact, however, one has only begun to deal with the sermon as a whole. As any reader of Hebrews will undoubtedly note, the bulk of Hebrews takes discursive, rather than narrative form; it is a complex and tightly woven theological argument, which regularly moves to the "exhortation" (*paraklasis*) of the congregation. The preacher does not simply repeat the story of Jesus. Nor does he or she move from that basic story to other stories in an effort to remain faithful to the narrative genre. Rather, beginning with and regularly returning to a narrative text—the story of Jesus—the preacher develops the sermon largely through non-narrative forms of speech. And therein lies the challenge for contemporary preachers.

In order to discern what the preacher of Hebrews is doing—in order to examine the complex relationship between story and discursive speech in the sermon—I turn to the work of Hans Frei and Richard Hays. Both of them, as I have argued in a largely overlooked section in my book, *Preaching Jesus*, have highlighted the ways in which discursive speech can be organically rather than artificially related to narrative text.[4] In so doing, Frei and Hays highlight the complex relationship between the story of Jesus and sermon form. In addition, they suggest a way of thinking about sermon form that moves beyond the exclusive poles of inductive versus deductive.

In tackling the complex relationship between narrative text and discursive sermon, Frei and Hays suggest that we need to think about two dimensions of narrative often ignored by homileticians: the *unity* of the story and the *logic* of the story. Whereas contemporary homileticians have focused primarily on plot, Frei and Hays suggest that the unity and logic of stories are equally important.

The first dimension to explore is the unity of the story. In examining the story of Jesus, Hans Frei highlights the narrative's unity through a distinction between two categories of identity

---

[4]See Charles L. Campbell, *Preaching Jesus: New Directions for Homiletics in Hans Frei's Postliberal Theology* (Grand Rapids: Eerdmans, 1997), 201-211.

description: "intention-action" and "self-manifestation."[5] According to Frei, the "intention-action" category refers to the specific sequential events in the narrative that cumulatively render the identity of Jesus. Through the cumulative, sequential interaction of character and incident over time the gospel narratives—Frei's particular focus—render the identity of Jesus. Frei's intention-action category thus captures what many of us normally think of as narrative: the movement of the plot shaped by character and incident.

Frei, however, also notes another dimension of the story of Jesus, which he highlights through his category of "self-manifestation." Through this category, Frei seeks to name the unity of Jesus that emerges in the entirety of the narrative. In the story of Jesus, Frei argues, we may discern the "wholeness" of Jesus, his persistence as a subject, and this way of identifying Jesus goes beyond the mere recitation of events. That is, through the interplay of character and incident, Jesus emerges (his self is manifested) as a unified character, about whom we can speak in ways that go beyond the mere retelling of the plot of the story.

In a similar way, Richard Hays, in his book *The Faith of Jesus Christ*, draws on the work of Northrup Frye to make this argument in relation to Paul's letter to the Galatians. Frye distinguishes between the *mythos* and the *dianoia* of narrative. *Mythos*, which parallels Frei's intention-action category, refers to the plot or linear sequence of events depicted in a narrative. *Dianoia*, which parallels Frei's self-manifestation category, refers to the "theme" of the narrative or plot examined as a simultaneous unity; it refers to the entire shape or pattern of the narrative that becomes clear in our minds. *Dianoia* seeks to capture the unity of the narrative elements—not merely the linear progression.[6]

---

[5]For Frei's discussion of these two categories of identity description, see Hans W. Frei, *The Identity of Jesus Christ: The Hermeneutical Bases of Dogmatic Theology* (Philadelphia: Fortress Press, 1975), 86-138; and "Theological Reflections on the Gospel Accounts of Jesus' Death and Resurrection," *The Christian Scholar* 49 (Winter 1966): 274-89.

[6]Richard B. Hays, *The Faith of Jesus Christ*, Society of Biblical Literature Dissertation Series 56 (Chico, California: Scholars Press, 1983), 21-23.

According to Hays, this move from *mythos* to *dianoia* shapes Paul's discursive argument in his letter to the Galatians. As Hays notes, a narrative substructure (a *mythos*, at times explicit, at other times implicit) underlies Paul's letter to the Galatians (similar to what I have said about Hebrews). Grounded in this narrative, Paul proceeds to expound the *dianoia* (the unity) of his story of Jesus in the form of discursive argument. Although grounded in the linear interaction of character and incident in the story of Jesus, Paul doesn't simply repeat that story. Rather, he interprets the unity and continuity of Jesus' person as a whole as that is rendered by the story. This move from *mythos* to *dianoia* (or, in Frei's terms, from "intention-action" description to "self-manifestation" description) provides one way of understanding a move from narrative text to discursive sermon in which narrative and discursive speech are organically rather than artificially related. That is, a discursive sermon may legitimately work with the *unity* of the story—the story as a whole—rather than simply dealing with narrative as a flow of sequential events.[7]

A second way of thinking about the relationship between narrative text and discursive sermon is through an examination of the *logic* of the story. According to Frei, the story of Jesus contains an internal logic which may be captured in the form of discursive speech or argument. For Frei, that logic involves a "pattern of exchange." It is a form of *narrative* logic because it is only intelligible through a sequence of events in which a hero/protagonist acts on behalf of others.[8] In terms of the story of Jesus, this logic goes something like this: In perfect obedience to God, Jesus vicariously assumes the guilt and literally assumes the *weakness* of humanity on the cross. Through his identification with humanity, Jesus vicariously exchanges his own moral purity for humanity's sinfulness and literally exchanges his own

---

[7]Hays, *Faith*, 20.

[8]In this essay I am dealing with two kinds of "narrative logic." Here I am concerned with the particular logic of the story of Jesus, which Frei and Hays refer to as the pattern of exchange. Later, I will discuss the characteristics of a broader narrative logic, which is distinct from both deductive and inductive logic. The logic of the pattern of exchange is only one type of this broader narrative logic.

strength for humanity's weakness. In the process he transfers his purity and strength to us. Jesus becomes a representative figure taking sin and weakness (death) on himself in order to set people free from them.[9] This logic, according to Frei, is inherent in the story of Jesus. Although intelligible only through a sequence of events, once discerned, this logic may be reflected upon in discursive forms. While always having to return to the story for the richness and complexity of Jesus, one may preach discursive sermons shaped by the logic of the story and still remain faithful to the story itself.

Hays makes a similar argument with regard to Galatians. He too highlights the logic of Paul's story of Jesus and, in fact, argues that this logic is the same "pattern of exchange" noted by Frei.[10] As Hays summarizes this logic in Galatians:

> The Messiah, in obedience to God's will, bears the curse and dies vicariously on behalf of others (3:13). Because of his faithfulness, however, he is vindicated by God and given life (3:11) and the inheritance of God's blessing, which had been promised to Abraham (3:16). In receiving this blessing/promise, he remains a representative figure: just as others received the benefits of his death, so also they participate with him in the inheritance, which they have "in" him (3:14).[11]

Because of his reliance on this logic inherent in the story of Jesus, Paul's discursive argument in Galatians, Hays claims, is organically related to the narrative substructure of the letter — the story of Jesus Christ.

In short, Frei and Hays argue that "there can be a continuity between the language of story and discursive language, that the relationship between the two can be, at least in some instances, organic, rather than artificial."[12] Contemporary homileticians, in posing story and discursive argument as radical opposites,

---

[9] Frei, *Identity*, 64-65, 122.

[10] Hays, *Faith*, 208, 258.

[11] Hays, *Faith*, 209.

[12] Hays, *Faith*, 20.

have paid inadequate attention to the insights of Frei and Hays. By taking seriously the unity of the story of Jesus and the *logic* of that story, preachers may move from narrative texts to discursive sermons in ways that remain faithful to the story of Jesus.

This move from narrative text to discursive sermon is precisely what happens in Hebrews. In fact, Hebrews gives us one of the clearest examples of this movement in the New Testament—and we might even say in the history of Christian preaching. As I noted earlier, Hebrews is shaped throughout by the story of Jesus; in Hays' terms, it has a "narrative substructure," which is at times explicit, but throughout implicit. However, the preacher of Hebrews discerns a unity and logic to the story of Jesus, which then shapes the preacher's discursive theological arguments in the sermon.

Briefly, I think the *unity* in Hebrews lies in the theological emphasis on Jesus as the mediator of a new covenant. In the overarching story of Jesus the preacher discerns a unity to the whole—that of Jesus as the mediator of a new covenant. At several points in the sermon, the preacher states this unity very clearly: 8:6, 8:8-12; 9:15; and 12:24. And the most extensive Old Testament quotation in the sermon comes from Jeremiah 31, in which the "new covenant" is proclaimed. Consistent with this sense of the unity of the story of Jesus, the preacher of Hebrews interprets that story through the figure of the high priest. Because of his role as mediator between the people and God, the high priest serves as the appropriate figure for capturing the preacher's understanding of the unity of the story of Jesus. Within this understanding of the unity of the story, the preacher engages in the theological argument of the sermon.

In a similar way, the preacher draws on an understanding of the *logic* of the story in developing the argument in the sermon. And that logic, as both Frei and Hays argue, is the logic of the "pattern of exchange." This logic is not only consistent with the unity of Jesus as the mediator of the new covenant, but is also appropriately linked to Israel's story through the figure of the high priest. To restate this logic briefly: through his identification with humanity, Jesus vicariously exchanges his own moral purity for humanity's sinfulness and literally exchanges his own strength for humanity's weakness. And in the process he transfers his purity and strength to us. Jesus becomes a representative figure taking sin and weakness (death) on himself in order to set people free from them.

A couple of examples from Hebrews indicate the centrality of this logic in the sermon. Regarding death, the preacher states the logic clearly in 2:14:

> Since, therefore, the children share flesh and blood, he himself likewise shared the same things, so that through death he might destroy the one who has the power of death, that is, the devil, and free those who all their lives were held in slavery by the fear of death.

Jesus identified himself with humanity and took death upon himself, so that we might be set free from the power of death.

With regard to sin, the image of Jesus as the high priest, who not only mediates between God and humanity but actually becomes the sacrifice itself, captures this same "pattern of exchange." The preacher of Hebrews states this logic concisely at several points. In 2:16-18, we read:

> Therefore he had to become like his brothers and sisters in every respect, so that he might be a merciful and faithful high priest in the service of God, to make a sacrifice of atonement for the sins of the people. Because he himself was tested by what he suffered, he is able to help those who are being tested.

Similarly, in 9:11-14 the preacher draws on the figures of the high priest and the Day of Atonement in developing this "pattern of exchange." Jesus becomes not just the priest who offers sacrifice for the people, but in fact the sacrifice itself. By taking the sins of humanity upon himself, Jesus vicariously sets people free (redeems them) from sin.

> But when Christ came as a high priest of the good things that have come, then through the greater and perfect tent (not made with hands, that is, not of this creation) he entered once for all into the Holy Place not with the blood of goats and calves, but with his own blood, thus obtaining eternal redemption. For

if the blood of goats and bulls with the sprinkling of the ashes of a heifer, sanctifies those who have been defiled, so that their flesh is purified, how much more will the blood of Christ, who through the eternal Spirit offered himself without blemish to God, purify our conscience from dead works to worship the living God.

In 9:26b-28, the preacher again summarizes this logic with reference to both sin and death: "But as it is, he appeared once for all at the end of the age to remove sin by the sacrifice of himself. And just as it is appointed for mortals to die once, so Christ, having been offered once to bear the sins of many, will appear a second time, not to deal with sin, but to save those who are eagerly waiting for him."[13] Jesus, once again, is presented as a representative figure who takes sin and death upon himself in order to set others free from them. At the heart of the story of Jesus, as these examples suggest, the preacher of Hebrews discerns and proclaims the logic of the "pattern of exchange." In so doing, the preacher of Hebrews presents a striking example of the organic move from the story of Jesus to discursive argument.

In moving from the story of Jesus to a discursive sermon, the preacher of Hebrews suggests several implications for contemporary preaching. First of all, Jesus is more important than sermon form. Story serves Jesus, rather than vice versa. While story is appropriately used to render the identity of Jesus in the New Testament, the genre of narrative is not an end in itself, but is meant to point to Jesus. It is more faithful to preach Jesus in discursive forms (for example, a three-point sermon) than to tell stories that never move the congregation to Jesus Christ.

Second, there is a complex relationship between narrative texts and the homiletical appropriation of them. The story of Jesus and discursive speech can be in continuity with each other; they can exist in an organic relationship, rather than an artificial one. While preachers must return again and again to the story itself, sermons can capture the *unity* and *logic* of the story without simplistically using narrative forms. Narrative

---

[13] See also 1:10-14.

texts don't always require narrative sermons. Again, the key is preaching Jesus, not using the genre of story.

Third, in drawing on the logic of the story of Jesus, Hebrews actually provides a model of preaching that moves beyond the false dichotomy of deductive and inductive preaching—the two alternatives often posed by contemporary homiletics. Hebrews does not begin with abstract, cognitive propositions, whether these are doctrinal propositions or some universal truths of reason. The logic of the sermon is not *deductive* logic that moves from cognitive propositions. Nor, however, does Hebrews begin with human experience, whether general human experience or personal religious experience.

The logic of the sermon is not *inductive*, moving from the particularities of experience to more general conclusions. Rather, Hebrews begins with and continually functions within a story—the story of Jesus. The logic of Hebrews works within the framework of this particular, contingent story—this word handed down in a particular community and tradition. This model of preaching involves discursive speech shaped by the logic of a particular, contingent narrative. The story of Jesus— not abstract propositions or human experience—provides both the warrants for the preacher's claims and the constraints on what the preacher will say. The preacher expounds the unity of the story—Jesus as the mediator of the new covenant—through a logic shaped by the story itself—the "pattern of exchange." This particular story becomes the ordering pattern for *both* thought and experience. The preacher interprets the concrete situation of the community of faith within the peculiar "narrative logic" of the story of Jesus.

The sermon of Hebrews thus suggests the importance of a broad "narrative logic" for preaching. Richard Hays has highlighted several characteristics of this distinctive kind of logic, which may inform our preaching today. First, as I just suggested, this logic does not involve "logical necessities"— truths of reason. It is shaped by the contingencies of the story of Jesus itself. Different interpretations of the unity of the story are possible, as the diversity within the New Testament itself suggests. One is not limited, that is, to Jesus as the mediator of the new covenant. This discernment of the unity of the story represents only one possible way of understanding it.

Similarly, different interpretations of the particular logic of the story are possible.[14] The pattern of exchange itself may be understood in a variety of ways (from substitutionary views of the atonement to Christus Victor interpretations).[15] And other specific logics may be discerned as well. In dealing with "narrative logic," we are not dealing with rigid syllogisms. Rather, we are concerned with the "fitness" of a particular logic to the story of Jesus.[16]

Second, discursive preaching shaped by this broad "narrative logic" will be rich with allusions to the underlying story.[17] Just as the preacher of Hebrews returns to the story in the fashion of a jazz musician returning to the "theme," so discursive sermons shaped by narrative logic will continually return to the story that shapes the logic, whether that is done explicitly or through regular, subtle allusions to the story. The "narrative substructure" that shapes the logic of the sermon will be implicitly or explicitly evident throughout the sermon. There will be a narrative dimension to such sermons, even if narrative does not completely shape the form of the sermon itself.

---

[14] This particular logic of the story of Jesus (a "pattern of exchange") is simply one form that the broader "narrative logic" might take in a particular story. "Narrative logic," as I noted earlier, is a broader term than the logic of the pattern of exchange.

[15] According to *Christus Victor* accounts of the atonement, God, incarnate in Jesus Christ, wins victory over the demonic powers of the world through his death and resurrection. Jesus endures the full force of the powers of death in the world, but ultimately defeats these powers and sets human beings free from captivity to them. For a classic treatment of the *Christus Victor* model of the atonement, see Gustaf Aulen, *Christus Victor* (New York: MacMillan, 1931). For contemporary treatments of the *Christus Victor* model, see J. Denny Weaver, "Atonement for the Nonconstantinian Church," *Modern Theology* 6 (July 1990): 307-323; and Gayle Gerber Koontz, "The Liberation of Atonement," *Mennonite Quarterly Review* 63 (April 1989): 171-192.

[16] Hays, *Faith*, 223-224.

[17] Hays, *Faith*, 7, 196.

Finally, this "narrative logic" is poetic and tensive. Again, it is not the logic of a syllogism that moves inexorably from proposition to conclusion. Rather, functioning within the framework of a story, such discursive speech, like that of Hebrews, will be poetic and tensive, rich and polyvalent. It will invite the participation and involvement of the hearers, rather than rigidly limiting and defining meanings. Although discursive, such speech will continue to include many of the characteristics of the narrative in which it is grounded.[18]

From Hebrews, then, we discover that the relationship between narrative text and sermon form is more complicated than many homileticians have suggested. Along with the preacher of Hebrews, contemporary preachers need to explore kinds of discursive speech that move neither "deductively" from abstract, cognitive propositions nor "inductively" from human experience, but rather operate within the narrative logic of the story of Jesus. As Hebrews suggests, the narrative unity and logic of the story of Jesus, rather than a simple consideration of genre, may provide the crucial connection between text and sermon, enabling the story of Jesus to function either as the substructure of a theological argument or as the center of a narrative sermon.

---

[18] Hays, *Faith*, 264-266.

3

Spirituality and Preaching:
Metaphors of the Journey

Richard L. Eslinger

The Community of "To the Hebrews"

Different communities of faith in Jesus Christ are shaped by their traditions, by their theology and liturgical praxis, their sense of mission, and by the distinctiveness of their cultural and social location. The spirituality of any one of these communities weaves together these dominant factors in their life together and their mission in the world; conversely, when one or more of these factors experiences a significant shift, the spirituality of the community, too, will undergo change. Among all of the communities revealed within the literature of the New Testament, perhaps there is no other that can be discerned as clearly as that of "The Hebrews." Our explorations of the issue of spirituality, then, begins with this analysis of the group of Christians to whom this homily is addressed.[1] Four core characteristics mark their community and will come to shape their spirituality. Each of these core factors invites some elaboration before we turn to the response of the preacher of this sermon "To the Hebrews."

---

[1] Recent rhetorical studies of "To the Hebrews" have led to a growing consensus that the work "appears to have been written with a view to oral delivery." David A. deSilva, *Perseverance in Gratitude: A Social-Rhetorical Commentary on the Epistle "To the Hebrews"* (Grand Rapids: Eerdmans, 2000), 35-36. Of course, in the ancient world, that assessment also extends even to explicitly epistolary documents (the Pauline corpus). Increasingly, however, interpreters of "To the Hebrews" now refer to the work as a homily or sermon rather than as an epistle. The Epistle "To the Hebrews "is really an early Christian sermon." Judith Hoch Wray, *Rest as a Theological Metaphor in the Epistle to the Hebrews and the Gospel of Truth* (Atlanta: Scholars Press, 1998), 1.

1. The profound break with the past.

Members of the community had been converted by a message "through the Lord," and "attested (or "confirmed) to us by those who heard him."(2:4). Both the content of the message and, in fact, the Messenger himself is "the Lord" (*tou kyriou*) (2:3) even though it may have been delivered to them by evangelists who had heard the kerygma directly from Jesus. The authentication of their word, then, is both that they were with the Lord and received it from him and that they had known the Lord in the words of the witnesses. As the Preacher[2] continues in the Hebrews homily, whenever he turns to admonish the community toward perseverance and reinvigorated faith, he intimates or directly refers to this authoritative Word that has given them membership in God's new people. The Preacher does not let this awareness of the Source of their new life remain long in the background! So, for example, the encouragement to hold fast to faith in 10:19-39, directs the community to freshen the memory of its origins in the Word: "But recall those earlier days…"(10:32). The break with the past in "those earlier days" was profound and world-shaking!

2. "The Awesome Rites of Christian Initiation."[3]

By the third century, the actual rites of the sacrament of Christian initiation are available, chiefly in the Apostolic Constitution of Hippolytus.[4] However, we may detect references to most every aspect of those rites in "To the Hebrews." In the sixth chapter, once again at the opening of a section of admonition, the speaker disclosed the journey by which these Christians

---

[2] With Thomas G. Long, we shall designate the author of this homily, "the Preacher." See Long's *Hebrews, Interpretation: A Bible Commentary for Teaching and Preaching* (Louisville: Westminster John Knox Press, 1997), 2-3.

[3] See Edward Yarnold, *The Awesome Rites of Christian Initiation: The Origins of the R.C.I.A.* (Collegeville: The Liturgical Press, 1994).

[4] See *Hipploytus: A Text for Students*, trans. Geoffrey J. Cummings, Grove Liturgical Study 8 (Nottingham: Grove Books, 1976).

were "made, not born."[5] They are admonished not to lay again
the foundation upon which their faith is built (6:1b). First in the
journey towards faith was "repentance from dead works" leading
to "faith toward God." (Later, the church would formalize these
as the *renunctio* and the *adhesio* in the baptismal liturgy — the
renunciation of Satan and the turning and adhering to Christ.)
Then is mentioned the time of instructions (6:2), dealing with core
matters of faith and liturgical practice. Within two centuries, this
season of instruction will have, first, a possible three-week shape
to its time of formation and by the fourth century, the familiar
contours of the season of Lent. Whatever the duration and
structure of this time of catechesis, the members of the Hebrews
community had become "enlightened" (*photisthentas*), entered
into the waters of their baptism, and received the Holy Spirit
(6:4). Once again, we see here early intimations of the later rites
of baptism followed by anointing and/or with the laying on of
hands (perhaps referred to in 6:2). These latter sign acts pointed
to the newborn Christian's reception of the Spirit. In every
tradition in Primitive Christianity whose practices we now have
before us, the newly baptized are immediately ushered into the
community and join with them in a first eucharistic celebration.

3. An early season of charismatic new life.

In "those earlier days," the members of the community had
experienced a most wondrous and varied outpouring of the gifts
of the Spirit. After their conversion, "God added his testimony
by signs and wonders and various miracles and by gifts of the
Holy Spirit, distributed according to his will"(2:4). The account
is remarkably similar to that given by the evangelist Luke in his
description of the events of the first Pentecost in the Jerusalem
church (Acts 2:1-4). Once again, these gifts and signs of the
Holy Spirit also served to underscore the sudden shift between
these converts' old life and their charismatic new life in Christ.
The converts "have been enlightened, and have tasted the
heavenly gift (eucharist?), and have shared in the Holy Spirit…"
(6:4). "This immediate presence of the divine," deSilva notes,

---

[5] Tertullian, *De Baptismo*. (The earliest treatise on baptism, written around
200 AD.)

"provided for a different experience of the world as far as the converts were concerned, such that the world could no longer be seen as objectively identical to what it was for the converts before initiation."[6]

4. The present crisis of persecution and shaming.

Now, those earlier days appear to be distant, past memories of a lost time of glory. The members are now encountering resistance from their former friends and neighbors and, most seriously, are being shamed for their faith. Even in those earlier days, they had "endured a hard struggle with sufferings, sometimes being publicly exposed to abuse and persecution and sometimes being partners with those so treated"(10:33). The Preacher to the Hebrews continues to name the tribulations that their persecutors have heaped upon them: imprisonment, confiscation of property, and physical abuse—though not yet "to the point of shedding your blood"(12:4). Perhaps more abusive than the physical pain itself, however, was the shame that derived from the public nature of this abuse. In those earlier days, even, they were exposed to public abuse. The admonitions in the homily point to the corrosive effects of this publicly administered shaming and abuse. Members are falling away from the faith they had received and affirmed, and even those who remain within the community are suffering from low morale and an erosion of hope and confidence. These conditions are the desired outcomes of those who persecute the community by abuse and by shaming. Their tactics are becoming ever more obvious and effective within the congregation(s). They have the prospect, in the words of John Wesley, of becoming "a dead sect."

5. Against the World: The Glory that is Christ.

Given the pastoral situation for the homily "To the Hebrews," several rhetorical strategies are available to the speaker. At the heart of it all, there is a desire that the little community turn from its present time of shame, defection, and hopelessness toward renewed faith in its Lord. The glory that is Christ Jesus,

---

[6] deSilva, *Perseverance in Gratitude*, 11.

of course, can, and is, asserted in its brilliant singularity and narrative drama. "Long ago," the homily begins, "God spoke to our ancestors in many and varied ways by the prophets, but in these last days he has spoken to us by a Son, whom he has appointed heir of all things, through whom he also created the worlds"(1:1-2). The entire first chapter, then, continues this recital of the glory that is Christ Jesus.

However, having performed this prologue, the speaker now has the challenge of shaping a rhetorical strategy that will lead the little flock to a renewed vitality in faith and hope. The strategy will be marked by a strong sense of mobility—after all, a new "re-conversion" to the faith is at stake—and by a prophetic recalling of the origins of the community on behalf of their present endurance and future rest in God. And through it all, the speaker will proclaim the ever-present glory that is Christ—Son of God, suffering Messiah, and High Priest forever. Specifically, the strategy that is chosen is the biblical motif of the wandering people of God.[7] The dire situation in the present is re-framed by way of interpreting their travail as like that of God's chosen people. They are, indeed, that people of God, and their wandering will be revealed to be that of a journey. It is a journey with Christ and to Christ. They will find their rest. Such a journey metaphor, of course, comes laden with its biblical imagery and narratives. That journey is the means by which God forms a collection of individuals to become God's covenant people. And all along the way, a question abides as to the virtues necessary to sustain such a community in the midst of an unbelieving and hostile world. The journey with God in Christ both leads the chosen people and forms them to embody personal and communal character in order that they can persist as sojourners until they find rest.

The journey begins as God graciously invites individuals into covenant, grants them the promises, and thereby forms them to be "the people of God," the *laos tou theou* (4:9). The communal character of faith is so compelling and encompassing

[7] Ernst Käsemann, *The Wandering People of God: An Investigation of the Letter to the Hebrews*, trans. Roy Harrisville and Irving L. Sandberg (Minneapolis: Augsburg, 1984).

that biblical faith is impossible for the individual by him-or herself. Käsemann remarks that it is "with a certain naivete [that] Hebrews seems to explain Christian existence by way of an illumination of existence as in fellowship."[8] The persistently communal context of the Hebrews homily may have appeared somewhat odd or naive to Käsemann, yet it was an essential act of re-framing the situation of the congregation(s) on behalf of their faith and even their survival.

However, this response of astonishment at the audacity of the speaker of the Hebrews homily will not remain only with this faithful German commentator (Käsemann wrote his commentary mostly while imprisoned by the Nazis in 1939). Such a pervasive communal context to the journey of faith will also appear naive, or even scandalous, to many of those who gather in our congregations week in and week out. These, our members and our friends, have been so formed by the individualism of American culture that in many respects, the message of Hebrews will remain opaque until translated into more one-to-one categories. Then, too, we need to confess that within the college of preachers, many come with this culture-formed bias that looks to most any text with the lens of pietism. These preachers will approach even the most communal text and seek only for selves without a world.[9] The project is, of course, to get these selves redeemed, or, in a more Romantic version of pietism, to get their hearts warmed and uplifted. However, for "To the Hebrews," such a project is doomed. To know the salvation of the Lord is to become a member of the wandering people of God. The solitary self cannot be construed as a model of piety for the Preacher. In fact, the opposite is the case. Those who have fallen away (6:6) now become as ground that produces only useless thorns and thistles. This soil, comprised of those who have forsaken the community, "is worthless and on the verge of being cursed..."(6:8). The hope

---

[8] Käsemann, *Wandering People of God*, 21.

[9] See Edward Farley, "Praxis and Piety," for his critique of this individualistic paradigm, in *Justice and the Holy: Essays in Honor of Walter Harrelson*, ed. Douglas A. Knight and Peter J. Paris (Atlanta: Scholars Press, 1989), 242-43.

persists, however, that for those willing to sojourn and wander together, God will form these selves into a people worthy of the promises. The greatest promise, however, is that the Lord will abide with the community in the journey until they have been fully formed as God's people and come to a glorious rest.

The Wandering of God's People

Viewed from a somewhat two-dimensional view, the logic of "To the Hebrews" might be depicted as having a horizontal plane (the wandering of God's people) and a vertical plane (Christ and Son and High Priest); the latter intersecting the former at strategic locations along the way. Within such a framework, we find numerous references to the gathering of a people who then are called/fated to wander among the nations. Called together by God, the people of the first covenant (9:1) sojourned by faith and were graced with divine blessing. The people of God received the promises and from the beginning, strove to fulfill them and obtain them. While many of the saints of the first covenant did obey the promises, beginning with Abel even before Abraham, none received the fullness of what had been promised, "since God had provided something better so that they would not, apart from us, be made perfect"(11:40). This motif of wandering, however, defined God's people as distinct from all other peoples and nations. As sojourners, the people of God would remain "strangers and foreigners on the earth" (11:13). Yet while the covenant people remained aliens among the nations, God's presence and provision were promised along the way. However, the speaker "To the Hebrews" presented this horizontal movement of wandering as being fraught with ambiguity. While the wandering implied a journey—i.e., with God and toward God's promised rest—the same metaphor could serve to express a rootlessness and discontent... even rebellion. Because of such rebellion and sin, the "journey" became, for forty years, an aimless wilderness wandering. None of that generation, the Preacher remembers for his hearers, entered the rest that was promised (i.e., the promised land). "So we see that they were unable to enter because of unbelief"(3:19). Wandering, therefore, could embody a profound and mystery-filled sense of God's-people-being-led. The same metaphor also can stand for God's-people-in-rebellion.[10]

Within this initial two-dimensional model, then, the vertical line of intersection represents the occasions of sacrifice within the first covenant by which the priest interceded for the people before God. At every location throughout the wandering, priestly ministers offered gifts and sacrifices to God on behalf of the people. These places of offering and the preparations and prerequisites necessary for those offerings are carefully documented by the speaker in chapter 9:1-10. Abel being the first, the line of priests and high priests within the first covenant all strove to effect this vertical intercession with God at some specific time and place of their wandering. However, the effort of these repeated acts of sacrifice did not yield the desired and decisive intercession. The offerings, "again and again," enacted "day after day," could never remove the sins of the people (10:11). Moreover, the priests were mortal and their mediation was momentary at best. So to the ambiguous motif of the wandering people of God is added the compromised motif of the sacrificing people of God. In both the horizontal and the vertical, there is that which is of God. Each, however, has been corrupted and ultimately does not succeed. The people of the covenant do not find rest; the sacrifices never remove sin and effect divine reconciliation.

It is at this point that the homily pulls the two-dimensional model into a new and multidimensional form. The two chief trajectories will remain, but each is transformed by the work of Christ. The wandering people of God are now given a new covenant, though with the same promises that had never been obtained before. The promises made to Abraham are true, but have remained unachieved. Now, for those whose faith is in Christ, they are being fulfilled. On one hand, the wandering motif is transformed into that of a journey. Here is a clear way to follow, since Jesus is "the pioneer and perfecter of our

---

[10] deSilva notes that the example of the wilderness generation serves "as an inductive proof by means of which the author hopes to demonstrate the reality and gravity of the danger of thinking too lightly of God's promises and not remaining firm in one's trust in God to provide what God promised." *Perseverance in Gratitude*, 141.

faith"(12:2). Paradoxically, the journey remains consistent with the ancestors in faith—Jesus "who for the sake of the joy that was set before him endured the cross, disregarding its shame, and has taken his seat at the right hand of the throne of God" (12:2). By the gift of Christ Jesus whose journey leads to the shame of the cross and only then to exaltation and great glory, God's people can lay aside their negative assessment of being shamed by the world. Contrary to any conventional or worldly wisdom, this abuse and shaming experienced by the community now serves to encourage faith and strengthen endurance. With their eyes set on the prize—of Christ at the right hand of God— the people of God can now journey together with faith and in hope. Christ is pioneer and forerunner. He has accepted the world's shame and removed its sting, which many of us know may be worse than the sting of death itself.

On the other hand, the same Lord has taken the vertical trajectory of sacrifice and offering and transformed it as well. What is revealed in this proclamation To the Hebrews is that all along, "we have a great high priest who has passed through the heavens, Jesus, the Son of God"(4:14). The vertical trajectory— *from* the people of God *to* God—could never take away sins. Its rites were corrupt and its priests mortal sinners. Yet the foundation upon which this vertical trajectory is based remains true. This foundation is that "without the shedding of blood there is no forgiveness of sins"(9:22). But a priest in the levitical succession could never achieve this atonement. Only a priest "according to the order of Melchizedek"(7:17)[11] is capable of a holy, once for all sacrifice for sins. Christ is the great high priest who enacts the new covenant and even better promises (8:6) for the faithful. So Christ is both priest and sacrifice, not at any earthly place of sacrifice but a "greater and perfect tent (not made with hands, that is, not of this creation)"(9:11). His blood, shed in that earthly place outside the city gate, is at the same

---

[11] Melchizedek is not of the order of Levites. "In fact he does not have a genealogy at all, according to the verse quoted in 7:3." George Wesley Buchanan, *To the Hebrews: Translation, Comment, and Conclusions* (Garden City, New York: Doubleday, Inc.,1972), p. 121. Buchanan also notes the superiority of Melchizedek even to Abraham whom he blessed in 7:6. *Ibid.*

time the perfect sacrifice in the Holy Place above the heavens. The ancient promises are renewed and new promises offered. A new people of God is born and begins the journey to that place above the heavens.

In this paradoxical way, therefore, the horizontal and vertical trajectories—God and God's people—are transformed in Christ. All of the old places of the wandering are merely shadows of the places that await those who journey together in Christ. And the old rites of the cult, along with the offices related to those offerings, are similarly disclosed as ineffectual. Nevertheless, the congregation of the Hebrews does not hear a message that infers all that has gone before is now obsolete and thus disposable. "To read Hebrews exclusively in this way...is to blur some subtle distinctions," Thomas Long cautions, "and finally to distort the relationship between the old and the new in the epistle."[12] To be sure, the old rites and places were sketches and shadows of the new covenant now begun by the great high priest, Jesus. Rather, the motifs and patterns of the old wandering people of God become earthly signs of the heavenly glory. They have become "outward and visible signs of an eternal and heavenly grace." Very much like sacraments, these places and rites are transformed to be places of meeting with the High Priest and sacrifice. In other words, there remains a people of God, but now of a new covenant in Christ. They are heirs to all the original promises made to Abraham, but also receive new promises through Christ's final and acceptable offering. God's people still wander outside the city gate, remaining strangers and foreigners on the earth.

Yet those wanderings are now revealed as a journey, taken first by Jesus, our pioneer. Even as high priest, his journey into the heavenly Holy Place is a model for our own journey and our own hope. Along the earthly way, however, God's people gather to offer praise and worship to their God and Sacrifice. There is a proclamation of God's mighty acts, just as in earlier times, though now fulfilled in Christ. (Recall that "To the Hebrews" may well be a sermon proclaimed to the assembly on the first day of the week!) And the "priest" and people make an

---

[12] Long, *Hebrews*, 12.

anamnesis of the one perfect sacrifice for the sins of the world
as they give thanks and share the Bread and the Cup of the
new covenant.[13] All is made new in Christ. Yet the structures
and patterns of the earlier covenant gain new and transformed
identity in the new.

Rest and the Journey

The metaphor of wandering is introduced in the sermon
as Jesus, "the apostle and high priest of our confession"
(3:1), is aligned with Moses who "also 'was faithful in all God's
house.'"[14] While the initial metaphor being developed is that
of a house (*oikos*), the Mosiac reference draws the Exodus and
wanderings of God's people into the foreground, beginning in
3:7. Now, with the metaphor of wandering under consideration,
the quote from Ps. 95:7b-11 (which itself refers to Num
14:23, 28-30) represents the first in a series of arguments "from
the opposite."[15] Because of the rebellion of the people, God's
wrath was stirred and a divine oath was uttered—"They will
never enter my rest"(3:11). Rest, in this initial depiction, is
obviously a reference to entering and remaining in the land
of Canaan. Wandering in the wilderness was opposition to rest
in the promised land, denied to that rebellious generation. The
Preacher now turns to exhort his listeners not to put themselves
in a stance against God similar to that of the wandering Hebrews,
"who sinned, whose bodies ("corpses") fell in the wilderness"
(3:17). In this exhortation of the listeners, however, we notice
that the image of "land" has been displaced by "rest."[16] Again,

---

[13] Most of the reformed eucharistic prayers no longer translate anamnesis
strictly as "remembrance." It usually takes a phrase in the text to speak of
this liturgical action. The United Methodist attempt at translation proclaims
that "whenever we break the bread and share the cup, *we experience anew*
the presence of the Lord Jesus Christ and look forward to his coming in final
victory." This anamnesis even leans forward to anticipate Christ's parousia!

[14] The text that the preacher is drawing on here is Num 12:7. See Buchanan,
To the Hebrews, 57.

[15] Wray, *Rest as a Theological Metaphor*, 62.

from the opposite, the Preacher adds that the divine oath was against those who were disobedient. It was these who "would not enter his rest" (3:19). "Land" is fading like the Cheshire Cat's grin; a more salvific and eschatological notion of rest is coming into focus. We should not be surprised, however, that this promise to the earlier covenant was unfulfilled and therefore that "the promise of entering (God's) rest is still open"(4:1).

At this point, the metaphor is expanded to encompass (1) sabbath as rest and then (2) the rest of God upon completion of the work of creation. By now in the course of the argument, rest has detached from land, leans forward as an open promise to the people, and harkens back to the great sabbath of creation. Having set an *urzeit* at creation, the *endzeit* of rest is now given as the eschatological rest of God's people, "for those who enter God's rest" and who also will be able to rest from their labors just as God rested on the seventh day (4:10). The two "bookends" of rest, then, are at the beginning and at the end. However, in between the times, the Jewish sabbath is set aside as the present tense intimation of those cosmic times of rest. By now, we would expect this from our preacher. The institution of the sabbath cannot contain the fullness of the rest now promised anew to the faithful people of God.

On the other hand, the speaker does not simply lay out the future hope of rest and move on to other issues. Rather, for the faithful people of God, rest is, in this sacramental sense, a possibility "today"(quoting Psalm 95:7b). Because the promises remain for God's new people, at the level of their life together along the journey, rest is an existential possibility. The metaphor, however, has expanded to what Judith Wray refers to as a "comprehensive theological system."[17]   The completed rhetorical unit dealing with rest in its skein of meanings (3:7-4:13) is distinctive among all of the imagery and metaphors developed by the Preacher to the Hebrews.

---

[16] Abraham J. Heschel has noted that for God's people Israel, the Sabbath represented this profound shift from a focus on spatially-related events to a celebration of time. See his *The Sabbath: Its Meaning for Modern Man* (New York: Farrar, Straus and Giroux, 1951), 12-24.

[17] Wray, *Rest as a Theological Metaphor*, 48.

The various meanings of rest are explored theologically and existentially, but their specific reference to Jesus Christ remains undeveloped.[18] Rather, while the metaphor of rest will not appear again in Hebrews, the theme of entering emerges with particular Christological force. Christ the high priest enters "the Holy Place." Returning to his central interest in the "journey" of Jesus Christ on behalf of his new people, the metaphor of rest becomes transformed into that of "entering into the sanctuary, into the heavenly Jerusalem..."[19] By way of this transformation, then, the motif of wandering once again reasserts itself over that of rest. So while the promise of rest "remains open," the issue now becomes the virtues and qualities of life in covenant that will allow the wandering people to finally enter the eternal rest of God.

Virtues of a Wandering People

Virtue is never solitary when it comes to the character sufficient to sustain a community in Christ through seasons and ages. Sustained by a living tradition, the church is formed to have certain virtues that befit the gospel.[20] In those times when a church settles into an easy, stable life, comfortable with itself and in conformity with its world, a certain cluster of more delimited virtues may be discerned: tolerance, civility, self-reliance, and respectability (interwoven, of course, with faith, hope, and love). But for a community that finds itself "strangers and foreigners on earth," the issue of the virtues sufficient for the journey becomes crucial. The church situation in post-Christendom America has, in a few decades of profound social change, become much like that of the community that has come to be named "The Hebrews." Now, and with some

---

[18] *Ibid.*, 83. Wray contrasts this lack of identification of rest with Christology in Hebrews with the well-known invitation by Jesus in Matthew's Gospel, "Come to me, all you that are weary and are carrying heavy burdens, and I will give you rest" (Matt 11:28).

[19] *Ibid.*, 84.

[20] See Stanley Hauerwas, *A Community of Character: Toward a Constructive Christian Social Ethic* (Notre Dame: University of Notre Dame Press, 1981).

urgency, we turn to interrogate the preacher of this homily with regard to the virtues necessary to sustain community in such a world. Suddenly, the metaphor of a wandering people of God seems no longer quaint and antique. We listen to the sermon "To the Hebrews" and remark to ourselves, "He's talking to us, too, isn't he?" So, as a critical issue of the spirituality necessary to sustain our faith outside the city gates of this world, we turn to the virtues in this proclamation. As we have come to expect, these virtues are largely assembled within the exhortations that are clustered throughout the homily. The core virtues essential for the journey include:

1. Boldness. The New Revised Standard Version translation of 10:19 reads "since we have confidence to enter the sanctuary by the blood of Jesus,..." Certainly, the metaphor of entering involves this quality of confidence. However, the choice of "confidence" as a translation is adequate, but perhaps unduly limiting as a personal and communal virtue. The word *parrēsia* connotes not simply confidence but outspoken boldness. Its literal meaning is "freedom of speech" and "it was used more widely to mean 'without fear,' 'freedom of action,' 'outspokenness," or 'power'...."[21] (If contemporary America spoke *koine* Greek, a number of vehicles would be sporting bumper stickers announcing, *Parrēsia!* instead of "No fear!") Boldness of speech, in this exhortation, is grounded in our confidence to follow our pioneer and high priest into the sanctuary through his work of sacrifice. Having made that journey—albeit proleptically while on earth—God's wandering people exercise a freedom of speech that may appear audacious to the world. More specifically, the man or woman called to preach within the wandering community in Christ in these

---

[21] Buchanan, *To the Hebrews*, 167. Also see Walter Bauer, *A Greek-English Lexicon of the New Testament and other Early Christian Literature, Third Edition*, ed. Frederick William Danker (Chicago: The University of Chicago, 2000), 782.

days is called to a "holy boldness" no longer best described "as one without authority."[22]

2. Memory. The speaker to the Hebrews admonishes his congregation much like the prophets of Israel did theirs...by way of inviting the community to remember the narrative that has brought them to the present time and place. "But recall those earlier days..." the preacher urges. Without a lively memory of how God has led us in ages past, hope for the community in the present is problematic. Certainly this issue speaks to churches that now seem to suffer a sort of adamant amnesia about the stories of the biblical narrative. In fact, one of our primary tasks as preachers at the outset of this new millennium is to deliver Scripture's narrative back to a biblically illiterate church. "But recall those earlier days..." is now an essential homiletical invitation.

3. Steadfast hope. The African American spiritual that became one of the theme songs of the civil rights movement was "Keep your eye on the prize, hold on." There is an interesting interplay of firm resolve and on-the-march purpose that combine in this virtue. Again in this core exhortation section of Chapter 10:19-39, the concluding verse urges the virtue "from the opposite." "But we are not among those who shrink back," announces the Preacher, "and so are lost..." (10:39). Turned right side up, the affirmation is that in Christ Jesus, we can hold steadfast to the hope that can empower us for the journey. Ironically, the Greek word for "steadfast (*bebaion* in 6:19) derives from a root meaning "stable" or "base." Yet that grounded hope precisely gives us strength for the journey. This metaphorical mismatch of "holding on" while on the march is fully apparent in 6:19. We have this

---

[22] Fred Craddock, *As One Without Authority* (Nashville: Abingdon, 1979). To be fair, Craddock was addressing an American church still living, and preaching, as if Christendom were a perennial condition. The bright exception to this perceived location, of course, was the African American church whose preaching has always been marked by the virtue of this boldness of speech!

anchor-like hope that makes us capable of entering the Holy Place following our pioneer and high priest. Yet the metaphoric clash is crucial for a wandering people. Too much emphasis on the "base" compromises the mobility necessary to follow Christ. But any attempt by God's people to journey without being grounded in the hope becomes just wandering in the wilderness. It is as if we need to sing *"My Hope is Built on Nothing Less"* at the same time that we also sing out *"Marching to Zion"*! "As we make bold to build on the foundation of (Christ's) word and friendship," deSilva adds, "we discover, as generations of Christians have found (cf. 13:7), just how trustworthy he is. We learn that obeying Jesus' call is not, in the end, a risk at all, but a sure foundation."[23]

4. Mutual love and compassion. "Let mutual love continue," exhorts "To the Hebrews"(13:1). Life in covenant cannot persist without this on-going, mutually-shared love. So the Preacher urges the community "to pour themselves into building up a strong community base and network of support for the individual believers, creating the kind of group that can sustain the commitment of its members, even when society brings its most fearsome weapons to bear on them."[24] Here is a community marked by *philadelphia*. Yet this love that is building up the community is not to remain only within it. Here, we see a striking contrast with present day "church families" that gather every Lord's Day and pray for each other but whose prayers rarely extend beyond the membership of the congregation. To the contrary, the community is to reach out in compassion, to those in prison and those suffering every kind of indignity and persecution. There is an "empathic imagination" at

---

[23] deSilva, *Perseverance in Gratitude*, 525.

[24] *Ibid.*, 485.

work in this kind of compassionate love.[25] The people of God are to be "bound together with" (*syndedemenoi*) those who suffer, literally being "partners" with them. The love of Christ must be at work within the church; it can never remain there.

5. Hospitality. It would be odd indeed if God's covenant people were not once again reminded of their covenant responsibilities to extend hospitality. The famous injunction that is also a promise urges, "Do not neglect to show hospitality to strangers, for by doing that some have entertained angels without knowing it"(13:2). Once again, we encounter a virtue of the people of God having a certain paradoxical character. "Brotherly" or "mutual" love rarely invites strong resistance from members of a congregation. This particular hospitality, however, is a love of strangers (*philoxenias*). Especially in the present American context, a current of xenophobia is welling up in the aftermath of the events of 9/11. The biblical injunction is enduring and its warrant compelling. We are to extend hospitality to strangers because we not only *were* strangers in our wandering past, but *remain* "strangers and foreigners on the earth"(11:13). For some churches, this exhortation regarding hospitality points to the need for welcome of the biblical narrative itself. Here is a profound disorder within some parts of the Body—a xenophobia toward the Word itself!

Other personal and communal virtues append themselves to this core cluster. However, for the preacher who addresses The Hebrews, the wandering people of God will need to travel light as regards the possessions of this world (another virtue—see 13:5) while carrying with them the virtues capable of sustaining a community of hope and compassion.

---

[25] Thomas Troeger's term for this personal and communal solidarity with those who suffer and are put down on society's margins. See my *Narrative & Imagination: Preaching the Worlds That Shape Us* (Minneapolis: Fortress, 1995), 102-09.

The Preacher and the Proclamation

If covenant, journey, and rest are the three essential motifs for the spirituality of the people of God, the spiritual formation of those called to preach will also be shaped by these metaphors. It may be the case as well that their significance even extends to the preacher's journey towards the proclamation itself. Simply put, our three motifs relate to the preacher *and* to preaching. Some initial exploration of covenant, journey, and rest as regards the preacher and his or her sermon might begin with the following ruminations:

Covenant. Is it always the case that preachers understand themselves to be part of the wandering people of God? From a pastoral perspective, this means, of course, a lived-out solidarity of the minister with the congregation. Viewed from another perspective, the issue of the covenant among those of us called to preach is at stake here. Have we become so infected by a worldly competition with each other that collegiality in our central vocation suffers? Do we speak only of church politics and retirement benefits when we gather, carefully avoiding Christian conversation about our ministry of proclamation? Thankfully, there is much evidence that a new sense of our being a "college of preachers" is on the rise, including but not limited to Internet sermon discussions, lectionary study groups, and the amazing, ecumenical growth in homiletic resources. We are in covenant in this ministry of proclamation. Just as the autonomous Christian is an oxymoron for the sermon "To the Hebrews," so, too, is an autonomous preacher.

With regard to homiletic method, we are reminded once again of the profoundly communal nature of most biblical texts. They address a communal consciousness[26] and we seriously distort their message and their intention by viewing them through the lens of individualism. One homiletical issue in particular can transform the covenantal world of the Scripture into a world comprised solely of individual selves—our illustrations. Notice the trend over the past several decades. Sermon illustrations have been growing into elephantine mega-stories that no longer

---

[26] See David Buttrick, *Homiletic: Moves and Structures* (Philadelphia; Fortress, 1987), 276-79.

function to illustrate any single meaning in the sermon.[27] (They bring too many meanings and pull the listeners into their world so thoroughly that the congregation remains lodged there.) A survey of these mega-stories—often expanding to one-third to one-half of the sermon's content—will disclose several traits: (1) they speak mainly of individual religion, (2) they are thin on grace and heavy on moralism and works righteousness, and (3) they embody "wisdom" derived more from culture than from Christ. No matter how communal our interest in the text's message and intent, if our illustrations depict mainly individual selves, the covenantal "base" is defeated. "To the Hebrews" invites us to employ personal and communal examples, images, and illustrations in our preaching. After all, we are members of and speaking to the people of God.

Journey. As the discipline of spirituality has been recovered in the churches, the metaphor of the journey has become a prevalent motif of self-imaging by those of us called to preach. It is no longer unusual for us to speak to each other about our "journey" as persons of faith and as preachers of the Gospel. We have been cautioned by writers and teachers in the field of spiritual formation that our journey is never solitary (covenant again), and that strength for the journey is available through all of the means of grace. From the perspective of the preacher to the Hebrews, our journey is both a communal one with the wandering people of God and one of personal formation in Christ. Moreover, it is a journey into the rich depths of the biblical narrative after the model of the Preacher himself. One certainty regarding the author of "To the Hebrews": we may not know his name or his address, but this member of the college of preachers has immersed himself deeply in Scripture. The Preacher "knows his Bible"! More to the point, he loves the Word. [28]

---

[27] See my "'Fwd., Fwd., Fwd.': Mega-Story in the Untaught Homiletic," *Journal of Theology* (CV 2002), 3-22.

[28] Robert Farrar Capon encourages us to this immersion in the Scripture: "You're supposed to be falling in love with the Word—with the Beloved in whom you're accepted—not proving that your interest in Scripture is intellectually respectable." *The Foolishness of Preaching: Proclaiming the Gospel against the Wisdom of the World* (Grand Rapids: Eerdmans, 1998), 62.

With regard to sermon method, the metaphor of the journey is widespread in contemporary homiletics. Eugene Lowry urges preachers to "do time" rather than "do space" in the pulpit. By this Lowry observes that "the category of time underlies the current homiletical interest in narrative, story, parable, and plot."[29] Clearly, our prior homiletical formation was spatial in nature.

Most of us were trained to think space and not time, unconsciously of course, when we sit down to begin sermon preparation. The result is that without conscious consent we immediately set about to order ideas.[30]

However, a Copernican revolution has occurred within the field of homiletics and within the preaching in the churches. The motif of a journey is embedded within most every approach to preaching advocated in the new homiletics that has burst upon the scene within the last three decades. So Lowry concludes that "a moving sermon is more like a trip that takes us from here to there through the medium of time—from now to then."[31] A sermon, we are learning, invites our listeners to come with us on a journey.

Rest. The metaphor of rest speaks a bold word of caution to us with regard to our spirituality as preachers. There does abide within our guild a temptation towards works righteousness that is revealed when we overhear colleagues bragging to each other as they display the wall-to-wall scheduling of their ministerial date books (or Palm Pilots, nowadays!). This "game" needs to be understood for what it is—such over-functioning and lack of self-care is not faithful discipleship but addiction. So the Preacher to the Hebrews comes to us with this not-too-subtle message: If the Almighty God needed a day of rest after the work of creation, how much more do we "frail creatures of dust" need some regular sabbath. It may not be Sundays that provide us with much of that rest. (The Lord's Day in the early

---

[29] Eugene L. Lowry, *Doing Time in the Pulpit* (Nashville: Abingdon, 1985), 7.

[30] *Ibid.*, 12.

[31] *Ibid.*, 13.

church was not seen as a rest day, but a work day—the time of the liturgy, "the work of the people.") However, we need our sabbath as a core spiritual discipline.[32] In fact, from the perspective of "To the Hebrews," to not pause for rest after our work is to strive to outdo our Creator!

Rest as a homiletical motif has implications both for our work of sermon preparation and for the homiletical plot itself. What those "Saturday night preachers" have not grasped is that a time of resting disengagement is a necessary second step in any creative process following an initial immersion in the work of creation. As we begin the process that will lead toward a specific sermon on a particular day, the first engagement with the text is not best approached by way of commentaries and Internet sermon sites. Rather, it is by way of *lectio*, that is, a journey begun by praying the Scripture. Following that prayerful immersion, then, is the necessary second step of distancing oneself and of rest. Then, there can be a reengagement, bringing all of the resources of interpretation to bear, along with the decisions regarding specific sermonic method.[33]

Within the sermon itself, there is also a place for the notion of rest or pause. Most of us have experienced the draining experience of sermons whose pace and intensity is unrelenting. Particular methods will couch this need for rest in various ways. David Buttrick[34] speaks of the pause between moves in his homiletical plot while Evans Crawford[35] lists the pause as an essential component in the African American preacher's rhetorical resources. However, the Preacher to the Hebrews also

---

[32] See Marva Dawn, *Keeping the Sabbath Wholly: Ceasing, Resting, Embracing, Feasting* (Grand Rapids: Eerdmans, 1995).

[33] See my *Narrative & Imagination*, 94-102, for an analysis of these stages of the homiletical imagination.

[34] "Closure is *crucial*," David Buttrick insists. Upon the effective closure of a move, there will be a pause before the next move is developed. *Homiletic*, 50-53.

[35] Evans Crawford, *The Hum: Call and response in African American Preaching* (Nashville: Abingdon, 1994).

reminds us that the goal of our proclamation is always the good news that God has spoken to us through a Son who is the High Priest and pioneer of our faith. Ultimately, our preaching will find its rest as we lead the people of God to a joyous rest in the Holy Place with Christ. So the notion of rest is a reminder that our preaching will finally name the grace that is Christ.[36] Just as the day of rest for God's people is filled with sabbath joy, so, too, our preaching is a journey that concludes in celebration and in grace. However, the dynamics of journey and rest for those of us called to preach are always located within the midst of the people of God, a people graced with virtues sufficient to sustain community and to persevere in gratitude.

Now may the God of peace, who brought back from the dead our Lord Jesus, the great shepherd of the sheep, by the blood of the eternal covenant, make you complete in everything good so that you may do his will, working among us that which is pleasing in his sight, through Jesus Christ, to whom be glory forever and ever. Amen (13:20-21).

---

[36] See Mary Katherine Hilkert, *Naming Grace: Preaching and the Sacramental Imagination* (New York: Continuum, 1998).

4

Walk On

The Song as Sermon in the Music of U2

Greg Stevenson

Many readers may find this essay a curious fit in a book like this, as it is neither a sermon nor an interpretation of Hebrews. Rather, this essay functions as a bridge between the interpretation of the text as represented in the first half of this book and the proclamation of that text represented in the second half by connecting both of them to the contemporary culture in which they reside. The best sermons are those that effect a dialogue between the world created by the text of Scripture and the world that the sermon's audience inhabits. Preachers recognize the necessity of engaging the cultural world where they and their audience live, but have often done so in one of two ways. They either attack the culture for its immorality and antagonism towards Christianity, or they mine it for sermon illustrations. What is often lacking is a true dialogue between the church and the culture. In the case of preaching, this is most unfortunate, because there are certain trends taking place in contemporary western culture that make the preacher's task more difficult. What preacher has not found himself battling the television or movie theater for his audience's attention, or discovered that members of the congregation are having their theology shaped more by the "Left Behind" novels or the rock group Creed than they are by his preaching?

The reality is that popular culture today is capable of holding its own with the best homileticians. The popular arts (music, film, art, literature, etc.) are a form of communication that convey cultural values and beliefs.[1] Popular culture preaches its values and assumptions to us constantly and in many forms. It attempts to persuade us to adopt its view of the world. Due to the conviction of many Christians that the culture's message and the church's message conflict, the church's response to the cultural message has traditionally been to go on the attack. Certainly a function of the church should be to critique popular culture in the light of Christianity, yet the actual result is more often a *separation* of Christianity from popular culture. Surrounded by the enemy armies of popular culture, many preachers adopt a siege mentality, confining their message within the walls of the church and only poking their heads out long enough to lob the occasional grenade.[2] The underlying assumption of these preachers is simply that the church proclaims the gospel message, while popular culture proclaims a worldly message.

This hermeneutic of suspicion goes both ways. A major shift has occurred in the relationship between Christianity and popular culture, which involves a rapidly increasing trend towards embracing spirituality while rejecting organized religion.[3] People want Christ without the church. They want God removed from the boundaries that the divisive and argumentative religious world has created for him.

My purpose in this essay is not to discuss the reasons for this trend nor to evaluate whether it is beneficial or harmful,

---

[1] For further reading on this see: William D. Romanowski, *Eyes Wide Open: Looking for GOD in Popular Culture* (Grand Rapids: Brazos Press, 2001), 60; Robert K. Johnston, *Reel Spirituality: Theology and Film in Dialogue* (Grand Rapids: Baker, 2000), 13-17; Michael Frost, *Seeing God in the Ordinary: A Theology of the Everyday* (Peabody, Mass.: Hendrickson, 2000).

[2] "The Simpsons" are one example of this common practice. Unable to get past the show's general irreverence and humorous perspectives on Christianity, many Christians attacked the show as an example of everything that is wrong about television and society. Others, however, who have examined more closely the real purpose of the show conclude the opposite. For instance, see Mark I. Pinsky, *The Gospel According to the Simpsons: The Spiritual Life of the World's Most Animated Family* (Louisville: Westminster John Knox Press, 2001).

[3] For some statistics on this trend and a discussion of it, see "Charting Unchurched America" *USA Today* (March 7, 2002), D1-2.

although I believe divorcing spirituality from community to be highly problematic. Furthermore, I am not suggesting that recognizing spiritual value or a sound theological message in pop cultural art forms is a justification of the lifestyles or beliefs of the artists. I am also not suggesting that legitimately destructive aspects of culture should be embraced. The problem has been, however, that Christians are so quick to condemn popular culture without truly attempting to understand it that they miss the value and wisdom that is often there. My purpose is thus descriptive. Through an analysis of what is occurring in popular culture, I hope to expose some of the implications of this trend for preaching.

One significant result of the separation of spirituality from organized religion is that people are open to addressing theological issues in new ways. They no longer view preachers as the primary dispensers of theology. We live in a technological and media-dominated world in which traditional methods of oral proclamation must contend with new forms of religious communication. Pop culture artists have found it increasingly attractive to cross the boundaries between the sacred and the secular. Ignoring centuries of church debate over how to communicate the sacred message to a secular society, some of these artists have paved new ground by using their respective secular disciplines to spark theological debate. In recent years, for instance, television has become a major voice in the ongoing theological conversations occurring in American society. To our discredit, many television shows like *Picket Fences*, *Touched By An Angel*, *The X-Files*, *Boston Public*, *Buffy the Vampire Slayer*, and *The Simpsons* have frequently raised more significant theological questions and sometimes provided more substantive answers than do we in the church. In some ways, the situation has been reversed as pop cultural artists will sometimes use their "sermons" to attack the church or will mine the Bible for illustrations in service of their own message.

The gauntlet has been thrown down and preachers cannot ignore it. There is an ongoing theological conversation occurring in popular culture and preachers need to become a part of that conversation. The reality is that most teenagers, college students, and young adults acquire more of their knowledge about Christianity from music, film, and television than from the church. As unfortunate as this is, there is also an opportunity here because many of these people begin to ask questions about God and the Bible because of things they have seen on television or in movies. The goal is not to attack popular culture but to *dialogue* with it...to test the spirits, in a sense. As with any good conversation, both sides may learn something. In fact, the purpose of this article is to provide one example of how popular culture has accomplished what preachers strive for — bringing the world of Scripture to bear on our culture.

Christianity, Culture, and Communication

Since the early days of the church, Christians have debated the relationship between the church and culture. On one end, Tertullian argued that loyalty to Christ involves rejection of most cultural expressions; on the other end, men like Justin Martyr argued for more interaction between the church and the culture. At the center of this debate is the question of whether God is present in culture and can communicate through culture.

This debate has continued into the present with Richard Niebuhr providing the classic categories around which contemporary discussion revolves. He suggests that the church takes one of three stances with regard to the culture: "Christ Against Culture," "The Christ of Culture," or "Christ Above Culture," the last of which, according to Niebuhr, may involve a synthetic, dualistic, or transformative approach.[4] The point is that our present debate over the relationship between the church and culture is not a new one, but part of a long-standing discussion within the church. This article represents merely one more voice added to the conversation.

Within the field of homiletics, another debate has been raging over the best method of communicating the gospel. Responding to the challenge of preaching to those who already know the story well, Fred Craddock suggests preaching indirectly. Rather than direct communication, which is about transferring information, Craddock, following Sören Kierkegaard, argues for

---

[4] H. Richard Niebuhr, *Christ and Culture* (New York: Harper & Brothers, 1951).

an indirect method that is about "eliciting capability and action" from the hearer.[5] Craddock correctly notes that much effective communication takes place indirectly and he points to popular culture (art) as an example.[6] One function of pop cultural communication is the attempt to change thinking and behavior by drawing an audience into a story or into the world created by a song. Within contemporary culture, the rock group U2 are masters at communicating spiritual and biblical ideas indirectly.

The Spiritual Context of U2

The members of U2 are lead singer Bono, lead guitarist The Edge, bass player Adam Clayton, and drummer Larry Mullen. They began their musical career together as teenagers in Dublin, Ireland in the late 1970s, culminating in the release of their first album (*Boy*) in 1980. From the outset, U2 used their music to express weighty social and theological issues typically ignored by the mainstream rock scene.

Early in their career as a band, three members of the group (Adam Clayton was and continues to be the lone holdout) embraced Christianity. They aligned themselves with a fundamentalist Christian movement known as the Shalom Bible group. It was not long before their budding rock career began to conflict with the rigorous demands of the Shalom group and with their own spiritual convictions. They questioned whether one could be a rock star and a Christian at the same time and whether the "show business" life was an honorable pursuit. The tension reached a climax around 1981, when the band nearly broke up over their inability to reconcile their faith with their rock music career. In choosing to stay together, however, they ultimately came to the conclusion that faith and rock and roll were not mutually exclusive and that they could use their music as an expression of their faith.

---

[5] Fred B. Craddock, *Overhearing the Gospel* (Abingdon: Nashville, 1978), 82. The indirect method is not without critics. James W. Thompson, although recognizing value in the indirect method, highlights several of its "shortcomings." *Preaching Like Paul: Homiletical Wisdom for Today* (Louisville: Westminster John Knox Press, 2001), 9-14.

[6] Craddock, 107, 111.

In severing ties with the Shalom group, U2 turned away from organized forms of Christianity, opting instead for a less structured means of spiritual expression. One cannot understand U2's separation of spirituality from religion, however, without an awareness of how the religious landscape of Ireland impacted their attitude. In Ireland, the animosity between the Catholic majority and the Protestant minority runs deep. In that context, religion was often used as a club. Thus, U2's experience growing up was that of religion as politics and power. Bono states that in Ireland "they force-feed you religion...It's about control: birth control, control over marriage. This has nothing to do with liberation."[7] Even more than most, Bono witnessed firsthand the kind of division and weariness that organized religion in Ireland could cause. His mother was Protestant and his father was Catholic. "I had a foot in both camps," Bono wrote, "so my Goliath became religion itself; I began to see religion as the perversion of faith."[8] He was not the only member of U2 to arrive at such conclusions. Guitarist The Edge has said, "All religion seems to do is divide. I'm really interested in and influenced by the spiritual side of Christianity, rather than the legislative side."[9] U2 understand their rejection of organized religion not as a matter of turning away from God, but as seeking the Spirit of God in other contexts. According to Bono, "when the Spirit leaves the church, then all you have left is religion."[10]

Thus, U2 stand as a prime example of the tendency among pop culture artists to separate spirituality from religion. Lacking the church as their primary context for spiritual expression and dialogue, U2 sought such a context in their music. U2's blurring of the line between the sacred and the secular in their music is clear from their recent "Elevation" concert tour (2001-2002) during which Bono was known to proclaim to the audience,

---

[7] *U2: The Rolling Stone Files* (New York: Hyperion, 1994), xv.

[8] *Selections From the Book of Psalms* (New York: Grove Press, 1999), x.

[9] *U2: The Rolling Stone Files*, 14.

[10] This quote comes from the VH1 special, "Rock and Religion," which aired repeatedly in 2001.

"This is church." He says such a thing because he believes that music, even secular music, can be a form of spiritual communication and, in some cases, even a form of worship. In a recent interview, Bono said, "Music is love...music is the language of the Spirit. It's how God speaks to us, and that is why it is so often trampled on...But...what it can be is something extraordinary that reminds you of what you can be, and it's a blessing, I suppose."[11]

The band members of U2 believe that Christian faith must express itself in social justice. Spirituality is not an end in itself, but a means by which one seeks to improve the lot of others in society, especially the oppressed. Thus, their own spirituality has led them to active involvement in several political and social causes, such as Amnesty International, War Child, and the Jubilee 2000 Coalition. For U2, music is about much more than entertainment. It is a means of reaching people, of communicating a serious message, and of addressing important social issues.

A primary source of U2's thinking on social justice is the Bible. The members of the band are biblically literate and the Scriptures have long influenced and informed their music. It is noteworthy that in the planning of a recent edition of the book of Psalms, the publisher asked Bono to write the introduction. The choice of a rock star to write an introduction to the Psalms would seem laughable...if it were anyone else. For Bono, the Psalms were an important part of his musical education, providing him with his "first taste of inspirational music"[12] and continuing to influence the language and style of U2's music. Bono the rock star was always taken by the figure of David who with his charisma, penchant for music, and tendency to dance in front of his troops was, to Bono, "the Elvis of the Bible."[13]

Nevertheless, when U2 write songs that address biblical themes or draw on biblical language, they do so indirectly. They

---

[11] The interview was conducted on May 25, 2001 at the MuchMusic studio in Toronto (http://www.muchmusic.com/transcripts/u2.html).

[12] *Selections From the Book of Psalms*, viii.

[13] *Selections From the Book of Psalms*, x.

rarely quote from the Bible directly, opting instead for weaving biblical themes and language into the fabric of the song.[14] In a 1987 interview, U2's drummer Larry Mullen said, "We don't want to appear to be flaunting our beliefs...you don't want it to look like some sort of lecture or gimmick. The music, the lyrics say everything the band has to say about their feelings."[15] This subtle use of biblical themes in their music has allowed them to address the social and theological issues that drive much of their thinking without alienating their base of secular rock fans who have no interest in spirituality.

In the song "Walk On" from their most recent album, *All That You Can't Leave Behind* (2000), U2 addresses the theme of faith indirectly. Faith is a consistent theme in the music of U2 since their second album (*October*, 1981). For Bono, faith is so entwined with music that when he talks about one he inevitably comes back to the other. In his introduction to the Psalms, he writes, "Explaining faith is impossible...Vision over visibility...Instinct over intellect...A songwriter plays a chord with the faith that he will hear the next one in his head."[16] In its presentation of faith, "Walk On" draws inspiration from Heb 10-12. I contend that in form, content, and function, "Walk On" resembles a sermon on Heb 10-12...a sermon in the shape of a song. As such, it reveals that those who stand up in pulpits on Sunday mornings are not the only ones out there preaching Hebrews.

Hebrews 10-12 and the Call for Endurance

Scholars have long acknowledged the sermonic nature of Hebrews.[17] The section from Heb 10:32 through 12:3

---

[14] An exception would be the song "40," which is essentially Psalm 40 set to music.

[15] "Rock Rebel: Part 2 - U2: For Those Who Have Ears to Hear" (www.rockrebel.com/solomann.htm or www2.youtwo.net/news_archives.adp ?newsid=12800).

[16] *Selections From the Book of Psalms*, vii.

[17] William H. Lane, "Hebrews: A Sermon in Search of a Setting" *Southwestern Journal of Theology* 28 (1985): 13-18. See also Thomas G. Long, *Hebrews*, Interpretation: A Bible Commentary for Teaching and Preaching (Louisville: Westminster John Knox, 1997).

highlights this and provides the context for our discussion of "Walk On." The book of Hebrews addresses Christians who have grown weary. Beaten down by the struggle of maintaining faith in a hostile environment, they are in danger of giving up and abandoning Christianity (2:1; 3:12; 4:1, 11; 6:4-6; 10:25, 35-39; 12:12). Hebrews is a sermon of encouragement designed to call its hearers to endurance. The *form* of this sermon involves an alternation between exposition and exhortation, with the sections of exposition laying out the basis for the exhortation to endure. Heb 10:32 to 12:3 follows this same pattern, containing two sections of exposition (10:32-34; 11:1-40), each of which is immediately followed by a section of exhortation (10:35-39; 12:1-3).

In terms of *content*, the first section of exposition (10:32-34) describes the suffering that the audience endured shortly after their conversion. The author notes that they were able to endure such suffering joyfully because they were looking forward to "better and lasting possessions" (10:34). Almost anyone can endure suffering if the duration is short enough; yet, it is when suffering goes on and on that weariness sets in. This appears to be the case here. Their situation has not changed much over time (they continue to suffer) but their attitude has changed drastically. They no longer accept suffering joyfully; in fact, it has become a threat to their faith.

After reminding them of their joyful response to suffering in their early days as Christians and that the source of that joy was their knowledge of a future reward, the author of Hebrews moves to exhortation: "Therefore do not throw away your confidence which will be greatly rewarded. For you need to persevere" (10:35-36). They must not turn back, he counsels (10:35). In this exhortation, the author of Hebrews not only tells them to endure but also tells them how to endure: "My righteous one will live by faith" (10:38).

This leads to the next section of exposition (11:1-40). The function of Heb 11 is to provide the source of endurance. Thus, the author begins with a definition of faith that is tailored to the needs of his audience. "Now faith is the assurance of things hoped for, the conviction of things not seen." This definition highlights as a central component of faith the ability to see spiritually what cannot be seen physically...or, in the words of Bono, "vision over visibility." The recipients of Hebrews used to have this kind of faith when they endured suffering joyfully because they had hope in better and lasting possessions. Now that hope had faltered because they took their eyes off of the goal.

The definition of faith provides the basis for the author's presentation of great figures from Hebrew history. These figures are chosen because they represent people who lived out that type of goal-oriented faith. They endured hardship and suffering on earth because their eyes were focused on a reward that cannot be seen. Abraham set out for a place he had never seen, but that physical place was not the real goal of his journey. He was looking "forward to the city that has foundations, whose architect and builder is God" (11:8, 10). Moses chose a life of suffering because "he was looking ahead to the reward" (11:26). Others, the author says, were seeking a homeland, but not one of this earth—a heavenly homeland (11:14-16). The key to the endurance of suffering, according to Heb 11, is keeping one's vision on the reward of a heavenly home.

Heb 12 then moves into another section of exhortation by picking up the metaphor of the race. Surrounded by witnesses, they are to "lay aside" every weight and every sin that hinders them and "run the race with endurance" (12:1). Thus, the *function* of Heb 10:32-12:3 is to encourage the audience to endure their suffering and not to turn back. Key to running this race with endurance is a faith based in the certainty of a heavenly home.

Walk On: The Song As Sermon

One of the songs on *All That You Can't Leave Behind*, "Walk On," is dedicated to a woman named Aung San Suu Kyi. To understand the words of this song, which is essentially an address to Suu Kyi, it is necessary to understand her background. Her father, General Aung San, was assassinated in 1947 as a result of his efforts to achieve independence for the country of Burma. Afterwards, the country came under the control of a brutal military dictatorship. As a teenager, Suu Kyi left Burma and attended schools in India and England, ultimately graduating from Oxford University. In England she married and had two children. Despite living overseas, Suu Kyi believed that one day her duty to the freedom of her people would call for her return home to Burma.

Then in 1988, she learned that her mother was dying back in Burma. After returning to be with her mother, she quickly became involved in the pro-democracy movement. Her activities on behalf of the National League for Democracy led to her arrest in 1989. Nevertheless, Suu Kyi's continued efforts to work for the freedom of her people, even under house arrest, won her the Nobel Peace Prize in 1991. In 1999, her husband, who remained in England with her two children, was dying of cancer. The Burmese leaders, seeing an opportunity to rid themselves of this troublemaker, offered her an opportunity to return to England. She chose instead to stay in Burma under house arrest, knowing that to leave would mean she would never be allowed to return. She could not turn her back on the cause of freedom. Despite a brief release from confinement in 1995, Suu Kyi remained under virtual house arrest from 1989 until her release in May of 2002.

At the time of the writing of "Walk On," however, Suu Kyi remained under arrest with no foreseeable prospect of deliverance. Her situation mirrored in many ways that of Hebrews' audience. Both suffered because of their beliefs. For both, their suffering was ongoing and the danger of it wearing them down was very real. Both were engaged in a marathon struggle, not a sprint. For both, their suffering could be relieved by simply turning back, whether that be a return to Judaism or a return to England. They shared the same danger that the weariness and fatigue of their race would weaken their resolve.

In "Walk On," the format and language of Heb 10-12 finds subtle expression. The plea for endurance in faith that occurs in Heb 10-12 is applied to a new audience and context. In doing so, U2 have crafted a modern sermon in musical form that is designed to encourage its audience (Suu Kyi) in much the same way as Hebrews.

The structure of "Walk On" follows the same pattern as that of Hebrews: the alternation of exposition and exhortation. The format of the standard song with its movement from stanza to chorus is tailor-made for such a structure. The song begins with a spoken-word introduction of exposition that also provides the title for the album (*All That You Can't Leave Behind*).

> And love is not the easy thing
> The only baggage that you can bring
> And love is not the easy thing
> The only baggage you can bring
> Is all that you can't leave behind

The ultimate context for this stanza is death. U2 takes the cliché of "what you can't take with you" when you die and reverses it, highlighting instead what you can't leave behind. Love, they say, is the only baggage that we can take with us. It is what transcends death and can't be left behind. This opening assertion reminds us of 1 Corinthians 13:13 in which faith, hope, and love are what outlasts all else, "and the greatest of these is love."

The song proper begins with a description of the weariness and despair that potentially threatens Aung San Suu Kyi in her continual struggles.

> And if the darkness is to keep us apart
> And if the daylight feels like it's a long way off
> And if your glass heart should crack
> And for a second you turn back
> Oh no… be strong

At the end of the stanza the exposition turns to exhortation. Bono counsels her not to be one of those who turn back out of weariness but to be strong and continue on. Bono's concern that she remain faithful despite the temptation to turn back mirrors that of Heb 10:39, which concludes that section of exhortation by encouraging its audience not to be of those who turn back and are lost, but of those who have faith and are saved.

The concluding exhortation of this second stanza ("be strong") leads into the chorus that forms the main exhortation of the song. This primary exhortation of the song is the same as that of Heb 12:1, which concludes the discussion of faith in chapter eleven by encouraging the audience to "run with endurance."

U2 here has changed the language of running to that of walking, likely for rhetorical effect. In the musical context of the song, "walk on" is more aesthetically compelling than "run on."

> Walk on, walk on
> What you got they can't steal it
> No, they can't even feel it
> Walk on, walk on
> Stay safe tonight   •

It is a plea for endurance, an exhortation not to give up but to continue the race. What gives this person the strength and endurance to "walk on" is faith, hope, and love. These are the things that endure, that can't be left behind, and that oppressors can neither "steal" nor "feel."

Following the exhortation of the chorus, the song returns to exposition with language more directly influenced by Hebrews.

> You're packing a suitcase for a place none of us has been
> A place that has to be believed to be seen
> You could have flown away
> A singing bird in an open cage
> Who will only fly, only fly for freedom

Following the song's description of the weariness that threatens Suu Kyi and the exhortation to persevere and "walk on," comes a more specific exposition of the source of that endurance: faith. What gave the Old Testament figures in Heb 11 the strength to endure was the faith that they were heading towards a "place" that God had in store for them; a place referred to as a "city" or a "homeland" (11:10, 14, 16). These heroes of faith knew that they were foreigners on this earth (11:13) and that they were heading home. This faith in a *place* God has provided is the foundation upon which the author of Hebrews builds his exhortation to run the race. U2 uses that same understanding of faith to make the same exhortation. Bono sings "You're packing a suitcase for a *place* none of us has been." When he then goes on to define the nature of this place, Bono employs the definition of faith from Heb 11:1, which states that faith is being certain of what cannot be seen. Thus

Bono sings that this place is one "that has to be *believed* to be seen." Seeing is not believing; rather, believing is seeing. It is "vision over visibility."

The statement, "you could have flown away," is a reference to Suu Kyi's opportunity to leave Burma and return to her family. Like a "singing bird in an open cage," she could have flown away and left her suffering behind, but she chose to stay and suffer out of a sense of duty and love, because she felt she could only fly for the cause of freedom. The song then shifts from this exposition to the exhortation to endure.

> Walk on, walk on
> What you've got they can't deny it
> Can't sell it or buy it
> Walk on, walk on
> Stay safe tonight

Again, the faith that one possesses cannot be denied, sold, or bought.

When one's race becomes unbearable, and one's arms begin to droop, and the knees become weak (Heb. 12:12), it is faith in a heavenly home that keeps one walking on. This "home" becomes the focus of the next section of the song, which alternates between exposition and exhortation.

> And I know it aches
> And your heart it breaks
> And you can only take so much
> Walk on, walk on
> Home…hard to know what it is if you've never had one
> Home …I can't say where it is but I know I'm
> going home
> That's where the hurt is
> And I know it aches
> And your heart it breaks
> And you can only take so much
> Walk on

Notice that the description of the unbearable suffering ("you can only take so much"), along with the admonition to "walk on," frames the discussion of "home." U2 understands the concept of "home" to be central both to the suffering that Suu Kyi feels and to the ability to endure such suffering. They imply different meanings for the term "home" here. In the first line, "home" appears to refer to Suu Kyi's lack of a real home here on earth. Deprived of a father at the age of two, raised and educated in different countries, and forcefully confined in her own homeland, Suu Kyi, the song suggests, has never had a real home. She is a stranger and a pilgrim on this earth. Then, in the third line, it says that home is also "where the hurt is." Ironically, as Suu Kyi is confined under house arrest, it is her "home" that is the focal point of her suffering. Sandwiched in between these references, however, is the key to faith as expressed in this song: "Home... I can't say where it is but I know I'm going home." In this way, U2 states that keeping one's goal focused on a "place"—a heavenly "home" that must be believed in order to be seen—is the essence of an enduring faith.

The song concludes with a final exhortation that relies on the language of Heb 12. When encouraging his audience to "run the race with endurance," the author of Hebrews first tells them to "lay aside every weight and the sin that easily distracts" (12:1). Those running a race cannot afford to be weighed down or distracted, so anything that hinders the runner must be discarded. "Walk On" ends with the same admonition. Anything in this world that holds one back and distracts one from walking on must be left behind. In contrast to the writer of Hebrews, U2 goes on to list some of those things which hinder.

> Leave it behind
> You've got to leave it behind
> All that you fashion
> All that you make
> All that you build
> All that you break
> All that you measure
> All that you deal
> All this you can leave behind
> All that you reason
> All that you sense

All that you speak
All you dress up
All that you scheme

With "Walk On," U2 has crafted a song resembling a sermon in form, content, and function. With regard to form, the juxtaposition of exposition and exhortation mirrors the format of the text of Hebrews with the exposition providing the basis for the exhortation. With regard to content, "Walk On" resembles an expository sermon on the text of Heb 10:32-12:1. The song even maintains the same rhetorical progression as the biblical text. At the beginning of the song comes a description of how Suu Kyi's situation is wearing her down, similar to the situation of the Christians described in Hebrews 10. The middle movement of the song then focuses on how faith in a "place" and a "home" provides the foundation for endurance, just as Heb 11 does. Finally, the song offers the same conclusion as Heb 12 with the exhortation to leave behind those things that hinder the race and to walk on. With regard to function, "Walk On" attempts to encourage a woman who finds suffering and opposition wearing her down and tempting her to give up. The overall purpose is to persuade. Through exposition, the song lays out the reason why and the means how this woman can endure. The ultimate goal is an exhortation to action: walk on.

This song accomplishes the hermeneutical move from text to sermon. "Walk On" takes an ancient biblical message and applies it to a modern context that parallels the ancient context of Hebrews, while maintaining faithfulness to the message of the text of Hebrews. It is a sermonic song addressed to one woman, Aung San Suu Kyi, but, by virtue of being released to the public, intends to be overheard by a much larger audience. Those who overhear the message of this song find in it an admonition to endure the hardships of life through faith. But as with any sermon, there is another element that affects how a sermon is heard: performance.

The Audience, the Sermon, and the "Preacher"

A sermon cannot be divorced from its audience and the setting in which it is delivered. Something happens in the presentation of a sermon, with its interaction between preacher and hearer, that causes the sermon to take on a life of its own. The circumstances surrounding the presentation of a sermon (time and date, the makeup, mood, and shared experiences of the audience) affect how a sermon is presented and how it is received. What preacher has not tried to deliver the exact same sermon in a different setting and to a different audience only to learn that doing so was impossible? Either the preacher discovered the need to alter the sermon in some way to fit the new circumstances or the preacher discovered that even if the sermon was delivered word for word, it was not received in the same way. The sermon became either more relevant to or more disconnected from its audience. The performance of a sermon (like the performance of a song) transcends the mere words of the sermon (or the lyrics on a page) as it engages an audience in a specific time and place. All these factors (sermon, preacher, audience, time, and place) create an experiential moment in time that cannot be replicated. To fully explore how "Walk On" functions as a sermon in the form of a song, it is necessary to discuss performance.

U2 recognizes that a song, like a sermon, is much more than words on a lyric sheet and notes emanating from musical instruments. The singer and the band communicate those words and notes through their own personalities. Bono hints at this idea in the context of his discussion of the Psalms. Building on his analogy of King David as the "Elvis of the Bible," Bono acknowledges the scholarly debate over whether or not David actually wrote all of the Psalms that have been attributed to him. Bono draws on his experience of the relationship between the singer and the song and how a singer can make a song his own through his performance of it, even though he may not have written it. Bono applies this understanding to the Psalms when he says that "it is not clear how many, if any, of the psalms David or his son Solomon really wrote. Some scholars suggest the royals never dampened their nibs and that there was a host of Holy Ghost writers... Who cares? I didn't buy Leiber and Stoller... they were just his songwriters... I bought Elvis."[18]

Of course, the limitations of this written format put us at a disadvantage. To engage the performance of a sermon or song, that performance needs to be experienced in a visual and auditory way that does not occur on the written page. Nevertheless, I want to discuss one performance of "Walk On" as an example of how a change in the audience and the shared experiences of that audience affected the presentation of the song.

As with the act of preaching, a musical performance involves a message, an audience, and a context. Thus, a change in the audience or in the context can necessitate a change in the message. On September 11, 2001, the terrorist attacks on United States soil generated a crisis of faith in this country. Suddenly Americans felt less secure, less confident, and less hopeful. Many of our own lay dead. The country was suffering, hurting, and in need of encouragement. Across the country preachers stood in the pulpits the following Sunday, trying to bring God's message to a hurting nation, trying to deliver a biblical message that could somehow make sense of what had happened and provide healing and comfort. U2 also saw in this situation a chance to "preach" a message of healing and hope. They took their song, "Walk On," and applied it to a new audience and a new context. In this way, they brought the message of Hebrews to bear on a nation's tragedy.

On September 21, ten days after the terrorist attacks, U2 took part in a nationwide, televised concert that was simultaneously broadcast on all major networks. It was an unprecedented moment in television history. U2's performance of "Walk On" contained three significant changes from the version appearing on their album, two of which were made specifically for this performance. First, they removed the spoken introduction and substituted a brief portion of another song off of the same album, a song titled "Peace on Earth." The irony of this choice is that the song was written in response to a deadly 1998 bombing in Omagh, Northern Ireland. For two decades, U2 had sung about the need for social justice and an end to violence and oppression. By the time "Peace on Earth" was written, it seemed as though

---

[18] *Selections From the Book of Psalms*, xii.

the band had become jaded and disillusioned. It was as though they realized that their hope for peace on earth was a pipe dream that would never be realized. The cycle of violence was indeed endless. The Edge somewhere commented that "Peace on Earth" ranks as one of the most bitter songs U2 has ever recorded. The song was written as a prayer to Jesus, asking for "peace on earth," but with a sense of hopelessness that such peace would ever be achieved.

The section of the song used as an introduction to "Walk On" is the beginning of the song, which states:

Heaven on Earth ...We need it now
I'm sick of all of this hanging around
I'm sick of the sorrow...I'm sick of the pain
I'm sick of hearing again and again
That there's gonna be Peace on Earth

In their performance of "Walk On," however, U2 made one alteration to these lyrics that completely changed their meaning. In the last line, they added the single word "never." Suddenly this song that had been a song about hopelessness became a song about hopefulness; this song of bitterness became a song of faith. Suddenly the new message of the song became "I'm sick of hearing again and again that there's *never* gonna be Peace on Earth." These transformed words of hope thus became the new introduction to "Walk On," appropriate words for a country in dire need of hope.

The two other changes made to the song during this performance occurred at the end. Bono is no longer singing to a solitary woman (Aung San Suu Kyi), but to a nation of people who are mourning their dead and looking for something to give them the faith and hope to endure. He thus focuses on the central message of Heb 11, which is that endurance and hope is grounded in the faith that God has prepared for his people a heavenly "home." In this televised performance, when U2 approaches the end of the song after announcing those things that are to be left behind, the band breaks out into a lengthy chorus in which they repeat one word over and over. That word is "Hallelujah" ("Praise the Lord").[19] As the band members sing out "Hallelujah" repeatedly, Bono shouts out the following words over their chorus:

> I'm going home!
> I'll see you when I get home!
> I'll see you when I get home!

Thus U2 offers up to a hurting nation a praise to God that is based in the assurance that God has provided a home. To the thousands who died in this tragedy, Bono affirms his belief that he will see them again and he counsels a nation to put their faith in the hope that only God provides. That hope is the source of our ability to "Walk On" in the midst of such a crisis.

The effect that this performance had on the nation was profound. In the weeks following this event, "Walk On" became a sort of unofficial national anthem that was frequently played on the radio and on TV news programs as images of the World Trade Center disaster site flashed on the screen. To a nation in despair, to a nation in danger of shrinking back, to a nation in danger of losing hope, U2 delivered a simple message of faith and hope from the book of Hebrews. That this message is delivered in musical form only strengthens its impact as the rational argument of the lyrics merge with the emotional appeal of the music to create a unique form of persuasion.

To suggest that a rock song can function as a sermon is not to say that it is superior to or more effective than a traditional sermon proclaimed in an assembly of worshippers. Rather, the point is that this is another method of preaching that is occurring in contemporary culture all around us, whether we acknowledge it or not. The performance of "Walk On" on September 21, 2001 was not done in a setting of worship. It was not a conventional sermon delivered in a pulpit on a Sunday morning. Yet, it was a sermon a nation needed to hear.

---

[19] The inclusion of the "Hallelujah" chorus first appeared on the single version of "Walk On."

II | Part 2:
Sermons on Hebrews

5

This is Our Story

Hebrews 1:1-4

Dean Smith
University Church of Christ, Austin, Texas

Introduction

Dean has spent the last three of his twenty-eight years in the pulpit preaching for the University Church of Christ in Austin, Texas. Dean also teaches ministry courses at Austin Graduate School of Theology. The following sermon demonstrates how years of experience, pastoral insight, and theological reflection can inform the crafting of a sermon.

This sermon strives to maintain the balance Luke Johnson describes between Jesus being fully human and fully divine. When preaching leans toward one over the other, often the result is the elimination of the role of suffering in the call to discipleship. In striving to maintain the balance, this sermon emphasizes the role of suffering as an important part of the process of coming to maturity in Christ.

This sermon also flows out of the story of Jesus and his sacrifice, which is, according to Charles Campbell, the story on which the Hebrews writer bases his sermon. Therefore, when reading "This is Our Story," look for Smith's allusions to the "narrative" logic in Hebrews.

This is Our Story

It opens with a series of pounding, percussive consonants meant to awaken the ear and quicken the heart and ends with a thunderous conclusion – "for our God is a consuming fire." Make no mistake about it – this isn't a letter ("Grace and peace from God our Father...") or a narrative ("On the first day of the week at early dawn..."). This is a sermon – a "word of exhortation" to a church that's weary and contemplating giving up; a church that's in danger of forgetting its story and losing its way. When a church is at this point it doesn't need more information or persuasive arguments. Even a letter from an apostle addressing specific problems misses the mark. The threat to a church like this isn't any one problem, but the accumulation of challenges and temptations and sacrifices that any church faces when it seeks to remain faithful to its calling.

This was a church that understood what it meant to be faithful. In earlier years they had joyfully suffered all kinds of persecution and loss for the sake of following Jesus (10:32f). It's just that for many of them the sacrifices seemed to outweigh the rewards and the expectation of any future, ultimate reward was growing dim. In short, they were tired. Thomas Long expresses it this way in his commentary on Hebrews.

> They are tired – tired of serving the world, tired of worship, tired of Christian education, tired of being peculiar and whispered about in society, tired of spiritual struggle, tired of trying to keep their prayer life going, tired even of Jesus...Tired of walking the walk, many of them are considering taking a walk, leaving the community and falling away from the faith.[1]

That describes some of us, doesn't it? That is, if our actions are any indication. Except for us, the struggle isn't against persecution or abuse – it's against boredom and a waning interest in anything associated with "church." You can see it

---

[1] Thomas G. Long, *Hebrews* (Louisville: Westminster John Knox, 1997), 3. I have read no other commentary on Hebrews that combines the best of scholarship with such a uniquely creative and thoughtful approach for preaching.

in the way we avert our eyes whenever someone is looking for volunteers; or in our growing impatience with others. You can see it in the way we straggle in to worship and complain about it when it's over. I don't read many church bulletins, but the ones I've read recently all seem to have the same theme – "not neglecting to meet together as is the habit of some..." (Heb 10:25). We're traveling more and assembling less. For a few of us this boredom expresses itself more subtly in a flurry of frenetic activity designed to keep us from having any time to reflect on our spiritual condition. It reminds me of the way the philosopher George Santayana once described a fanatic who "redoubles his effort when he has forgotten his aim."

The problem for us, as it may have been for them, is getting us to admit this. Because if we could admit it we could deal with it honestly and even seek help. Perhaps then we would realize that such fatigue is understandable, given the nature of our commitment. That following Jesus isn't a burst of spectacular activity as much as it is a marathon of consistent effort. Endurance, not speed, is what's required...and focus. Focus on the one who called us to this task in the first place. Focus on the one who went before us; the one who not only knows the way, but is the way. Look to Jesus, "the pioneer and perfecter of our faith," the preacher of Hebrews admonishes, but sometimes that's hard to hear for those who think it's just a call for more effort with less strength. After all, these people had never seen Jesus. They were at least a generation or two removed from the first disciples and the original events. They couldn't *see* anything, they could only *hear*. And so he preaches the story of Jesus – not so much to inform them, but to refocus their attention on the one who understood their struggles and interceded on their behalf.

For most of us, everything seemed so fresh and new when our journey of faith began. We felt so close to Christ and so full of faith and power. Every challenge, every sacrifice was met with enthusiasm and obedience. That's the way it was for these Christians. They could look back to a time when the way seemed so clear and the sacrifices they were called to make seemed insignificant in comparison to the transformation of their lives and their future. But soon those early days were behind them and the challenges of following Jesus in a hostile culture were beginning to take their toll. They began to weary from the sacrifices and feel the burden of their message and the hostility that it aroused. How would they persevere in the midst of such adversity? How would they find the Sabbath rest promised by God to all who were faithful? According to the preacher, their only hope was to rediscover it in Jesus.

Like any good sermon, this one has a text from which it draws its message and its power. And the message here is the very heart of the Christian faith: the story of Jesus, the Son of God, who sacrificed his life to purify us from sin. It isn't as elaborate as the "Christ hymn" that the apostle Paul offered in his letter to the church in ancient Philippi (Phil 2), but it has the same basic elements. Jesus, the Christ and Son of God, left the heavenly realm to become a human being and face all the temptations and struggles inherent in being human. God raised this same Jesus from the dead, after his suffering and death, and exalted him to God's right hand. Reading the two, side by side, we can almost hear the refrain of that old gospel hymn: "This is my story, this is my song / praising my Savior all the day long."

It's a sermon that reminds us that the one we follow was not only sent from God, he is God. He bears the "exact imprint" of God's nature, "upholding the universe by the power of his word." This is not some intermediary, like the angels or prophets of old. God has spoken his last word, his authoritative word, through the Son who sits at his right hand. It is the voice of God proclaiming, as he did at the transfiguration of his Son on earth, "This is my Son, the one that I love, listen to him!" (Mark 9:2-8). "See that you do not refuse him who is speaking," the preacher warns (Heb 12:25).

And yet this one who is fully God is also fully human. He who sits at the right hand of the "majesty on high" has also condescended to live our everyday experience. He who speaks a word on our behalf understands the power of temptation and the depth of human weakness. Who else but him could be the perfect high priest for us? He was the one who even "learned obedience through the things he suffered" (Heb 5:8) so he could become both the perfect example and the source of salvation for us. Although the preacher refers to him by many names and titles, his favorite is the one that reminds us of his solidarity with us: Jesus.

When the price for faithfulness rises, as the preacher assures them that it will, and "the shedding of blood" (Heb 12:4) becomes a real possibility, the only ones who will remain will be those who are "looking to Jesus, the pioneer and perfecter" of faith (Heb 12:2). And although it seems like a terrible thing to tell those who are already tired and discouraged, the preacher refused to calm their anxiety by forfeiting his obligation to prepare them for the future. The escalating persecution of Christians confirmed the wisdom of his courageous decision.

Every student of history can recall the dark days in England when Winston Churchill, who had for years warned of the Nazi threat, was finally appointed Prime Minister. His first speech, a radio broadcast on May 13, 1940, came just after his appointment. It was a memorable one. Who could ever forget his words on that occasion? Although he assured his fellow citizens that that the goal was victory – "victory at all costs, victory in spite of all terrors," he didn't even pretend that such a victory would be swift or painless. England had suffered enough with such naïve optimism. Remember what he said? "I have nothing to offer but blood, toil, tears, and sweat. We have before us an ordeal of the most grievous kind. We have before us many, many months of struggle and suffering."

In a similar manner, the preacher of Hebrews refused to discount the truth, either of what they had suffered, or of the suffering they would have to endure in the future. But he offered them more than just the prospect of additional sacrifice and loss. He offered them the life and the presence of the one who endured their temptations and struggles and even death itself that he might be both the one who saved them and the one who sustained them to the end. And by so doing, the preacher says, this one offered them the opportunity to grow and become the people that God had created and redeemed them to be.

Yet for us it's not so much the rigors of following Jesus, but the routines, that challenge us. The daily disciplines of prayer and study, devotion and service seem so mundane, so ordinary that we are often lulled to sleep spiritually and drift away from them without even realizing it. Day by day we excuse our neglect by blaming our busy schedules or our seemingly unlimited options to simply do other things. And then one day we awaken to face some real threat or danger and struggle to find the spiritual resources to respond faithfully. September 11th of last year was just such an occasion.

Now this week we will remember the tragic events that took place in New York City, Washington D. C. and on Flight 93 outside Pittsburgh, Pennsylvania. Let's face it, at a time like this it's difficult for any of us to look at those who committed such evil deeds, or those who would support them, with anything other than a desire for vengeance in our hearts. And from what I've been hearing over the last year, many Christians are struggling with those same desires. They're tired of being restrained against such unrestrained violence. They're tired of being admonished to love our enemies and pray for those who would abuse us. And they're certainly not interested in hearing anything about "turning the other cheek." Revenge? Yes. Reconciliation? Not on your life.

So where does that leave us? Is there another way to respond? Is there another story we can accept and follow? Certainly there is. Alternative stories abound and most of them involve heroic battles that result in our complete domination and victory. Even the Bible can be a resource for stories like that. But our story, the story of Jesus, revolves around the one who gave his life to break the cycle of hatred and violence in the world. By refusing to "return evil for evil" he sought to "overcome evil with good" (Rom 12:21). He came to earth to give his life to be Savior and Lord of all nations, not just one. Someday good will triumph over evil…someday. But until then, whether we like it or not, even if it seems too difficult to accept, the story of the cross is our story and *it must shape our response.*

Having said this, I wonder if you'll be back for the next installment of this sermon. You may decide, like some the preacher addressed, that it's just too difficult to follow Jesus. You may even visit another church where the preacher has learned to speak of discipleship in a way that makes the path seem painless and the outcome more certain. Or you may decide to hear him out, in spite of being wary and weary, because he knew the story of Jesus and was brave enough to proclaim it. Are you brave enough to hear it?

6

Fascinated by Angels?
Hebrews 1:5-14

John York
Woodmont Hills Church of Christ,
Nashville, Tennessee

Introduction

For over two decades John has preached for churches in
Oregon, Texas, and Tennessee. With a PhD in New Testament
from Emory, John uses his training to teach New Testament and
Preaching at David Lipscomb University in Nashville. He also
serves as one of the preaching ministers at Woodmont Hills
Church of Christ.

One of the few places in Hebrews that has an immediate
connection to modern interests is the discussion of angels. This
sermon connects our modern fascination with the interests of
the preacher in Hebrews and tries to carry through with his
demonstration that Jesus is the superior revelation of God. In
writing this sermon John incorporates ideas from Luke Timothy
Johnson regarding the Christology of Hebrews and the author/
preacher's understanding of Scripture as the living Word of
God. Too often in our own times, Scripture is more historical
artifact than living word. Popular spirituality and the current
fascination with power sources beyond ourselves make the
preacher's claims about the Christ a relevant word in our time.

Fascinated by Angels?

Admittedly, we don't know much about the author of
Hebrews and his audience. From the exhortations and style
of writing, we know this is more sermon than epistle. We
don't know who his audience is. We don't know exactly what
circumstances produced the sermon. We do know that the author
knows Scripture very well, and that he believes Scripture is the
living word of God. We know that he perceives in his audience
a tendency to lose sight of what God has done in Christ to bring
about their salvation. Social pressures, sometimes to the point
of persecution and suffering, have them confused. Some already
have lost faith, or at least lost interest in the community of faith.
Others don't seem to remember why this salvation of theirs is
that important. It is not that these people do not have spiritual
interests. Apparently they have quite an interest in life outside the
human realm. The author doesn't question their belief in angels,
for example. He embraces that belief, and that connection is his
starting point. After his attention-grabbing opening sentence, he
strings a series of quotations from Scripture designed to make a
point about the superiority of the Son of God to angels.

As I read through this text this week, I realized how foreign
this opening chapter is to my own world. Yes, I know we now
live in a time in which our culture in general has taken a great
interest in angels. You can buy them anytime of the year now,
not just at Christmas. I know about all of the television shows
spawned by *Touched by An Angel*. While I've enjoyed a variety
of movie portrayals of angels through the years, those portrayals
made them more unreal than real. Angels, as one recent
commentator put it, "have always lain at the edge of Christian
faith, and not at its center."[1]

What I know about angels can be summed up in less than a
paragraph. Angels are messengers from God, occasionally sent
by God for the protection of his creation. Some are described
as guardians or protectors of us humans. But if they show up

---

[1] Fred Craddock, "Hebrews," *The Interpreter's Bible*, Vol. 11 (Nashville:
Abingdon, 1998), 31.

at your door, watch out! If it's Gabriel, you don't want to hear what he has to say. If it's Michael, hell is breaking loose and the war already has begun.

But as I said, our author and his audience take angels very seriously. They understand that God's heavenly messengers have been sent in the past for the protection of humans. They understand that in the past God even delivered his Law through angels. They understand that in the scheme of created order, there is God, then angels, then humans. Near the end of his appeal, the author reminds his audience to "show hospitality to strangers, for in so doing some have entertained angels with out knowing it" (13:2). Our author believes that humans need to pay attention to the superior beings in creation. Angels are, by nature, closer to God than we are. He also believes his audience may be too interested in those intermediaries. More importantly he believes that in these last days, God has broken through that creation order. God has made himself, for a little while, lower than the angels. God has provided for humans in a new way that angels could not. He has provided a new protection that angels cannot provide. So the author begins by affirming the wonder of God's messengers in order to affirm an even greater truth about God's latest activity in his son. Notice as we read through this section the way in which he understands Scripture as present tense, as a current word from God.

> For to which of the angels did God ever say, 'You are my Son; today I have begotten you'? Or again, 'I will be his Father, and he will be my Son'? And again, when he brings the firstborn into the world, he says, 'Let all God's angels worship him.' Of the angels he says, 'He makes his angels winds, and his servants flames of fire.' But of the Son he says, 'Your throne, O God, is forever and ever, and the righteous scepter is the scepter of your kingdom. You have loved righteousness and hated wickedness; therefore God, your God, has anointed you with the oil of gladness beyond your companions.' And, 'In the beginning, Lord, you founded the earth, and the heavens are the work of your hands; they will perish, but you remain;

> they will all wear out like clothing; like a cloak you
> will roll them up, and like clothing they will be
> changed. But you are the same, and your years will
> never end.' But to which of the angels has he ever
> said, 'Sit at my right hand until I make your enemies a
> footstool for your feet.' Are not all angels spirits in the
> divine service, sent to serve for the sake of those who
> are to inherit salvation? (Heb 1:5-14)

In the space of nine verses by our count, the writer quotes
nine different Old Testament texts, six of which come from
the Psalms. It is God who speaks, not the individual Psalmist.
There is a single theme that is voiced: It is more valuable to pay
attention to what God has done in these last days through a son
than to get too carried away with an interest in angels. It's not
that angels are bad—they're part of God's heavenly entourage.
They are indeed messengers sent forth to serve. However, the
son is served by the angels. In fact, the son is seen to be part
of God himself in verses eight and nine, participating in the
creation of earth and heavens. In verses eleven and twelve, the
son remains the same when all else in creation changes.

"Therefore," chapter two begins,

> we must pay greater attention to what we have
> heard, so that we do not drift away from it. For if the
> message declared through angels was valid, and every
> transgression or disobedience received a just penalty,
> how can we escape if we neglect so great a salvation?
> It was declared at first through the Lord, and it was
> attested to us by those who heard him, while God
> added his testimony by signs and wonders and various
> miracles, and by gifts of the Holy Spirit, distributed
> according to his will (2:1-4).

The preacher looks back with his audience on the days in
which this great salvation was proclaimed, first through the Lord
himself, then through those who heard him. They can remember
the days of signs and wonders and gifts of the Holy Spirit,
distributed according to his will. All of those signs announced
a salvation that has come and is yet to come. There is a not-yet

side to this salvation that the preacher holds out in front of his audience. It is the "world to come," he says in verse five. More is at stake than protection from angels in this life. More is at stake than the present age. So he continues in the next section by telling the rest of the story about God the son, the first-born of all creation who himself was involved in the creation of all else in the universe. Being superior to angels, "for a little while" he took on the status of us humans.

Now God did not subject the coming world, about which we are speaking, to angels. But someone has testified somewhere, "What are human beings, that you are mindful of them, or mortals, that you care for them? You have made them for a little while lower than the angels; you have crowned them with glory and honor, subjecting all things under their feet." Now in subjecting all things to them, God left nothing outside their control. As it is, we do not yet see everything in subjection to them, but we do see Jesus, who for a little while was made lower than the angels, now crowned with glory and honor because of the suffering of death, so that by the grace of God he might taste death for everyone (2:5-9).

It is this last point (in verse nine) that for our preacher is the ultimate news of salvation. God has acted in the son to become human and then be crowned once more with glory and honor "because of the suffering of death, so that by the grace of God he might taste death for everyone." As he goes on to explain, the salvation that has come means ultimate victory over the great enemy of human existence: death itself. Angels can bring messages from God to humans, they can fight heavenly battles for humans, they can protect human life from death at times, but they can't overcome death. That is what God has now accomplished by becoming human with us. He is the pioneer, the champion of our salvation, the preacher says, and he was made perfect through suffering. He became just the right fit for our need, this preacher says, by sharing in our flesh and blood. He became like us "in every respect" so that he might become the ultimate intermediary between us and God, able to make us holy when we are not, able to help us times of trial. Listen to this last section of chapter two from Eugene Peterson's translation in *The Message*:

Since the children are made of flesh and blood, it's logical that the Savior took on flesh and blood in order to rescue them by his death. By embracing death, taking it into himself, he destroyed the Devil's hold on death and freed all who cower through life, scared to death of death. It's obvious, of course, that he didn't go to all this trouble for angels. It is for people like us, children of Abraham. That's why he had to enter into every detail of human life. Then, when he came before God as high priest to get rid of the people's sins, he would have already experienced it all himself—all the pain, all the testing—and would be able to help where help was needed (2:14-18).

"Therefore, we must pay attention to what we have heard, lest we drift away from it." The author of Hebrews probably would not know what to think about life in Nashville, Tennessee in 2002. He would not know what to think about our infatuation with football or major league baseball. No doubt he would be amazed at the various means of transportation available to us. Doubtless he would be amazed by the creature comforts that seem to be givens in our time: light and heat and air conditioning and water, heated or chilled to our liking. He probably would be amazed at how neatly we have compartmentalized our lives into secular and sacred, my time and God's time, my stuff and God's stuff. He would know about cosmetic efforts to fix our appearance, but probably be surprised at the ingenuity and economic status of our efforts to maintain appearance and youthfulness.

He would doubtless be amazed at the technology and skill and medical understanding that makes it possible to push back sickness and death and dying, to beat disease, to hold onto human existence as we do. But after taking all of that in, would he not look at us all and say, "Yes, but there is still death itself; still that which is more inevitable than taxes." He would still remind us that, no matter what comfort we might find in our belief in angels sent from God to console and protect us, angels cannot conquer the ultimate enemy of human existence. Only the Son of God has done that. Only the son has championed our cause and led the way through human existence, suffering death in the process. Only the son has returned to glory and promised to bring us to glory with him. Only the son knows what it is like, in every respect, to be human, so that he can come to our aid in every circumstance. "Therefore we must pay closer attention lest we drift away from so great a salvation." How distracted have we become?

7

The Bible in the Hands of an Angry God
Hebrews 4:12-13

Ronald Cox
Rochester College, Rochester, Michigan

Introduction

Ron offers the following perspective on his sermon: "This sermon is not part of a series on Hebrews and so presupposes the congregation has little working knowledge of the content and argument of the document. I first attempt to provide a context for the congregation, both in terms of Hebrews and in terms of themselves. The underlying function of the first part of the sermon is to name the barriers to hearing the Word of God: the preacher, the listener, and the surrounding world. The second part of the sermon, which places these barriers in perspective, deals with the writer's subject, the Word of God. This part functions as a line-by-line meditation on Heb 4:12-13 as a means of identifying the Word which gave the *Hebrews* writer pause. The goal of the sermon is to provide the congregation a basis for appreciating the Word of God so that they might take more seriously the message the writer received from it: 'Today, if you hear his voice, do not harden your heart.'

"Luke Johnson speaks to how Hebrews calls its readers to a path that will result in their transformation into 'genuine children of God.' The hallmark of such children, as exemplified by Jesus, is 'the obedience of faith that progressively opens us up to God's fearful freedom.' Hebrews 4:12-13, which describes the Word of God as a sword able to open us up before God, finishes a section that describes the prospects of such faithful obedience and the consequences of its absence (Heb 3:7-4:11, see esp. 3: 18-19 and 4:2). The possibility for such obedience came both to those who perished in the wilderness and to those ('us,' 4:2) who hear the good news now by means of a divine speech act (see 3:7, 15; 4:3, 4, 5, 7, 8). Verses 12 and 13 themselves deviate from what precedes by bringing this speech act ('the Word of God') to the foreground (and not focusing on faith, rest and punishment). These two verses reveal, if only for a moment, the machinery that propels both the author's 'word of encouragement' (note how the divine speech act is infused into the author's own from 1:1-2 to 12:25) and the transformation he seeks."

The Bible in the Hands of an Angry God

"Today if you hear his voice do not harden your hearts."
Today.

Today, I'm faced with the challenge of proclaiming this text, one which, oddly enough, I have chosen for this morning. Knowing I would be faced with this text today, I set out my *lexica* and my commentaries and my Greek text and my translations; I have all those there on my desk. And I began to work through this passage and this book. To prepare, I call upon my training and my learning. And I remember the genre of Hebrews, that Hebrews is unique in all the New Testament because it is one long sermon. Oh, it looks like a letter at times, but it is really just a very, very long sermon. Its style is the most superb Greek in all the New Testament, except, perhaps, for Luke and Acts. The language of Hebrews is intricate and delicate and beautiful and complicated.

I recall how much I personally enjoy Hebrews because it combines worlds of thought. On the one hand, Hebrews is very Greek in that it is so philosophical. It has a lot of Platonic imagery. On the other hand, Hebrews is very Jewish, dwelling on Israelite history and worship and especially on Scripture. It combines these for a singular purpose; the purpose of Hebrews is faithfulness.

So I set these things out, and I lay out my texts, and work on them so that I can know what I am doing, so that I might be able to speak to you right now, so you might hear me today.

Today, she sits in her pew, and she wonders, "Will he hear it?" So often she's argued with him: "what do you believe?" Almost all the times she's praying for him. Every time she reads the Bible, she thinks, "Oh, if he could only just hear this, it speaks right to him. If he could just hear this." Every time she listens during a Sunday morning sermon, she thinks not about herself, but about him. "Will he hear it? If only he would listen," she worries.

Today has enough problems of its own. Actually, today is not a bad day; in fact, it's a pretty nice day and we need to go out and enjoy it, especially since tomorrow, Monday, it will be different. There will not be much reason to relax then as we sit and we worry under the hot office lights and the glare of the boss and her strange, inane expectations. And we worry about the news from all around the world, and how it will effect, not only the global markets, but our local supermarkets: how it will effect sales and product parts procurement, how it will affect donations. And what does the latest news mean for our future? My future? Your future? We worry so much today about things that go on five thousand or ten thousand miles away.

Yet, today I am afraid we are unaware of what truly faces us. We are unaware of what is in our presence. Something very terrifying, my brothers and sisters, is afoot. And I'm afraid that we are not clued in to it. It's more terrifying than what we see and hear from the world around us; its more terrifying than our culture, which throws at us everything from images of Brittany Spears and Ozzy Ozbourne—and that's the light stuff—to endless news stories detailing this culture of death and how it permeates and disrupts everything from cradle to grave, reaping its fruit in our high schools and in our prisons, our hospitals and our workplaces. Today, right here, something is afoot that is more frightening than the outside culture's immorality, and even—may I say it—more frightening than our own immorality.

Something is afoot that is so terrifying the Hebrews author sees it and stops in the middle of his argument. He digresses in order to point it out for us. This digression looks like a praise, but don't be fooled; it is a warning. If you have your Bibles with you, take them out and look at them; eye them with suspicion as you consider the preacher's words: "Indeed the word of God is living and active. Sharper than any two-edged sword, piercing until it divides soul from spirit, joints from marrow; it is able to judge the thoughts and intentions of the heart. And before him no creature is hidden, but all are naked and laid bare to his eyes." That most terrifying thing is this Word of God.

I'm not trying to be rhetorical. I'm not making this up. Maybe this is beyond my skills to communicate, but I believe it with all my heart, that what is most frightening is what confronts us, you and me, this morning in Holy Scripture. It confronts us every time we pick up a Bible to read it. It confronts us every time we sit in a pew or in a Bible class and listen to it.

Think about what he says here; ruminate with me on these words for a minute, "The word of God." If the purpose of Hebrews is to engender faithfulness, the means that the author of Hebrews uses is to turn again and again to the Word of God. He is most concerned about what God says, as he makes clear at the very beginning: "Long ago, God spoke to our ancestors in many and various ways by the prophets, but in these last days he has spoken to us by his Son." Over and over again he quotes Scripture. Over and over again he talks about what God has to say to us today.

And the writer believes God's speaking to us is good news, that this is gospel; yet he also believes, as his summation shows, that this is a dangerous event, this speaking of God. He recalls in Heb 12:19 long ago on Mount Sinai, where a voice was heard whose words made the hearers beg that not another word be spoken to them. And he proceeds to say that there is a voice that speaks today that is far more frightening than what the Israelites experienced at Mount Sinai. In Heb 12:25, he says:

> See that you do not refuse the one who is speaking. For if they did not escape when they refused the one who warned them on earth, how much less will we escape if we reject the one who warns from heaven? At that time, his voice shook the earth. But now he has promised, 'Yet once more I will shake not only the earth, but also the heaven.' This phrase, "yet once more" indicates the removal of what is shaken, that is created things, so that what cannot be shaken may remain.
>
> Therefore, since we are receiving a kingdom that cannot be shaken, let us give thanks by which we offer to God an acceptable worship with reverence and awe. For indeed our God is a consuming fire.

Our God is a consuming fire. And his voice (the voice that speaks to us this morning from Holy Scripture) shakes the firm foundations of our created world.

This is the Word of God that the Hebrews writer must face and must present to those who need to hear the gospel. And he knows, he warns them, "The word of God is living and active."

There is that tired image, of course, of the dusty family Bible on the coffee table. According to that image, we just sort of set it over there and we don't pay attention to it. I actually am an admirer of those types of family Bibles. The first Bible I ever read was a big, thick, white, bonded leather family Bible on my grandmother's coffee table, next to the picture of Jesus with the sacred heart. And that was just the beginning of a life filled initially with infatuation for Scripture and then, eventually, terror. Still love, but a terrifying love.

In my profession, what we tend to do is to take Scripture out and use our lexica and our commentaries and our Greek text and our translations and all our education, and take pieces of Scripture and put some over here and some over there, claiming that we are setting it in its context. And pretty soon we have a dissection board where Scripture is laid out like a dead, inanimate, ancient object. Like an archaeologist laying out pieces of a mummy.

But we are mistaken when we do that. Just as are those who proof-text their way through Scriptures or use concordances without stopping to think what those individual verses are a part of; just as are those who think the Bible is only a blueprint or a map or a guidebook. The Bible is so much more than this. It is living and active. It is not static; it is dynamic. It moves to counter every move that you could make. It is not predictable, this Holy Scripture of ours. It is wily, agile, cunning, crafty.

"Sharper than any two-edged sword." I find this claim to be ironic. We hand out the Bible and that for us is a mark of piety—and it is a good thing. We want people to read the Scriptures—but we want them to know what they are getting. It intrigues us, how the Gideons (for instance) hand out little green-bound New Testaments. They do it at Rochester College. They did it at Notre Dame. They do it, I'm sure, at your workplaces. They hand them out, saying, "Here, have a Bible." What would you do if I were standing outside handing out knives to your children? The Scriptures are not some benign thing we can just hand out and say, "Here." Scripture is a dangerous, possibly even violent, weapon. There should be a warning label. This is much more hazardous to your heart than anything you eat, smoke, or drink.

At the same time this Word is not a club we go out and beat people with. It is not some crude instrument. "Piercing until it divides soul from spirit, joints from marrow." It reminds me of what a very sage person once said. His name was Obi-Wan Kenobi and he was talking to young Luke Skywalker. He gave Luke his father's light saber, and as Luke turns it on, old Ben Kenobi says the saber is not as clumsy as the blaster; it is a more elegant weapon from a more civilized age.

And Scripture, even though it is sharper than any sword we could imagine, is a delicate instrument, a refined instrument that can pierce through things we ourselves cannot separate, like soul and spirit. It is like a scalpel. And you would think that because it's so sharp and yet so refined, so delicate an instrument, so precise, that we would spend more time developing the experience and the expertise that we need to use this dangerous and powerful tool; that we'd spend more time preparing for it.

But I'm not sure we could prepare for it. Because, you see, "it is able to judge the thoughts and intentions of the heart." And if anything should give you pause, it is this. The Word is able to see right inside each one of us. It can pierce through whatever defense you can put up, whatever façade you can design, whatever you can construct to hide who you really are. Scripture can cut through that and unveil your heart. That's a scary thought. How many times have we opened up our Bible with thoughts that were not right, not stopping to think that even as we read, we ourselves are being read? How many times have we sat there in our comfortable pew, on the outside looking like we were listening but inside thinking things, wondering things, planning things that would cause us great shame if those around us knew? And all the while, Scripture knows exactly what we pretend to hide. That's a very frightening thought.

But it's also frightening to think who wields Scripture. Oh, we think we do. We think this is our sword. And in a sense it is. I don't want to ignore what Paul says in Ephesians 6, how the Word is the sword of the Spirit. We think, "We've got the sword." We're ready to do battle. We're ready to go out thumping people with our spiritual club. We're ready to lay waste to any argument that comes up against us, because we have our Bibles. We think that we wield the Scriptures. For good or ill, we think that.

But in truth, we do not. The sword of God is held by none other than God. Consider what the writer says: "before him no creature is hidden." This is a move away from what he's been speaking about, because now we're not talking about the Word, we're talking about him, we're talking about God, the one who holds the Word. And now we're not talking about the heart, we're talking about creatures. What are creatures? I pondered over that until it dawned on me. I'd forgotten. We're the creatures. We're the created things. See, so often we pretend, and we think that we are gods—that we are not creatures. And then we pick up this divine instrument and we think, we honestly think, that we have the stamina and the sagacity to wage war with this divine sword, this sharp instrument that is the Word of God.

But, you see, God became a man to reveal to us the truth that we are not gods. We are just human beings, and not very good human beings at that. And that is the scary thing—because the instrument that can cut through and pierce and reveal our heart, reveals it to God. All creatures—all of them—"are naked and laid bare to him." The imagery is frightening, and it's embarrassing. It's like being at the doctor's office, and you're there in all your glory, standing in front of him. And being naked, in front of a doctor, that's frightening, that's embarrassing. But imagine standing before God, not being able to hide anything. How humiliating. And that's exactly where we are this morning. Do not pretend to be anything but exposed to the living God right now. Exposed to the Almighty God, your creator, who sees you "laid bare."

The Greek word behind "being laid bear" has to do with the neck, giving the impression that the sword is right there at your neck. We are standing there with a sword, the divine sword in God's own hand, at our neck. Yet thankfully, this is not a war image, but a sacrificial image. The sword is there to render the animal, the created thing, a sacrifice to God.

And that's the image he leaves us with, before the Hebrews author moves on with the rest of his argument, the image of us standing right here, today, with the Word of God, the sword, the sharp, double-edged sword of God at our neck. And we're naked, and we're laid bare to him: God seeing even into our hearts.

And that's where we are left when we come to Scripture. Yet as terrifying as this is, I firmly believe this is a good place to be. What we do to protect ourselves, to hide ourselves, the devices we employ to disguise the reality of who we are, those need to be cut away. We need to stand before God as we truly are. Because then, and only then, will God truly heal us and make us clean, and make it so that we can have freedom and confidence in his very presence.

So now you can better understand the words of the psalmist. "Today if you hear his voice, do not harden your hearts."

8

Our Compassionate High Priest

Hebrews 4:14—5:10

Rubel Shelly
Woodmont Hills Church of Christ,
Nashville, Tennesee

Introduction

Rubel has preached for the Woodmont Hills Church of Christ in Nashville since 1978. During that time, he has also taught at David Lipscomb University and Vanderbilt University School of Medicine. He is author of more than twenty-five books.

The worldview of Hebrews is quite foreign to most modern Christians. And one of the unique features of Hebrews, as Luke Johnson points out, is the explicit assignment of the role of priest/high priest to Jesus in this material. This sermon provides both biblical background and a contemporary setting to help hearers grasp some of the central significance of this important theme. The Christology of the preacher's material cannot be grasped apart from it.

Our Compassionate High Priest

When I was a boy growing up in west Tennessee, I entertained the fantasy belief of every little boy about his father. My daddy was the strongest man alive. My daddy was the best man in the world. My daddy was the wisest of men and knew the answer to any question my mind could frame to ask. But every little boy thinks that about his dad. Right? Then we grow up and find out....

It was different in my case. As I grew up, I came to realize there were men with more brute strength than my father. I met and studied under people who had more degrees and academic accomplishments than he. And I met people who had far greater resources to do more good things that blessed people and made their lives better. But I will confess that I have never lost the sense that my daddy really was the strongest, wisest, and best man I have ever known. He remains my ideal of godly manhood to this day. At my best, I'll never be half the man he was.

But do you want to know the very best thing of all about James Shelly? *I lived in his house as a member of his family, his youngest son!* I held him in the highest regard, but I wasn't afraid of him. He was an incredibly busy and hard-working man, but he was never too busy for me. Why, his face would light up if I came into his office or plopped down by him when he was relaxing with a newspaper at home. Any one of his three sons had dibs on his attention, his time, and his heart. We never doubted it. Our relationship with him was different from anybody else's. We were his children. He loved us as he loved nobody else.

I sincerely believe that my relationship with that strong, wise, busy, good, and benevolent man has shaped my image of God immeasurably. And I got to tell my father that before he died! It has helped me understand that the Creator God of the Universe is my Loving Heavenly Father who wants all his children to know that his face lights up when we seek him. It has helped me frame a vision of Jesus Christ. My Redeemer, Sovereign Lord, and Great High Priest is not distant, detached, and disinterested. He is the Son of God who was subjected to every weakness and frustration the rest of God's children experience – and who cares for, understands, and helps us in our weakness.

The Preacher's Christology

The writer of Hebrews had an exalted view of Christ. He is superior to angels, greater than Moses, and far above Joshua. He is, after all, God's own Son who made purification for sins and is now seated at the right hand of God (1:1-3). He is a merciful and faithful high priest who made atonement for the sins of the people in service to God and has the ability to help us in our trials (2:17-18). He is the faithful Son over all God's house (3:6). He is the one alone who can give God's Sabbath-rest to those who believe in him (4:9-10).

If he is so high and holy, *can* he pay attention to our needs? Or is he like Aristotle's god, who is absorbed in the perfection that is himself? If he is greater than and superior to all others, *would* he be moved by the plight of those to whom this preacher was speaking? Or is he able to look upon the frail human condition only with contempt and loathing? If we grant that our High Priest Jesus is *able* to help us, do we have any reason to think he is *disposed* to do so?

This preacher affirmed that the high-priestly ministry of Jesus was being performed with great compassion toward and with full understanding of the human condition. He believed that Christ's sympathy for us grows out of his experience in the Incarnation. So, to people who needed to be encouraged to hold on when they in fact felt like giving up, he gave a strong encouragement for them to hold fast to their Christian commitment and to know that they would not be abandoned to or destroyed by their suffering. The temptation to turn back from one's commitments in the face of severe stress – even persecution – is something Jesus understands.

Therefore, since we have a great high priest who has gone through the heavens, Jesus the Son of God, let us hold firmly to the faith we profess. For we do not have a high priest who is unable to sympathize with our weaknesses, but we have one who has been tempted in every way, just as we are – yet was without sin. Let us then approach the throne of grace with confidence, so that we may receive mercy and find grace to help us in our time of need (4:14-16).

The Almighty God who is at the center of the cosmos wants us to "approach the throne of grace" where he is enthroned, and he wants us to do it "with confidence." Oh, how we would like to believe this! The One on the throne surely has the power to help us! But, like Isaiah of old, we know we are unclean people with unclean lips (Isa 6:1ff). How dare we move in the direction of that holy space? How dare we dream of "storming the gates of heaven" with our pleas and prayers? Indeed. That is why the Lord created the intermediary role of high priest in Israel. On the annual Day of Atonement, the high priest would go through the veil into the Holy of Holies and sprinkle the blood of sacrifice on the mercy seat. Once the blood was in place, mercy (i.e., sparing the people from the punishment they deserved) could be extended. More than that, on the merits of sacrificial blood, grace (i.e., showering the people with blessings they could never deserve) could flow from the throne. It took a consecrated high priest with consecrated blood in hand to make these things possible.

The role of the high priest in the Old Testament is impressive. He intercedes with Yahweh on behalf of the nation. He wears special robes. He functions with great ceremony and solemnity. The sight of the high priest on a holy day when you were feeling anything but holy could be daunting – unless you saw beneath the robe and ceremony a neighbor, a real human being like yourself, a friend, a kinsman.

That's why I began this sermon by telling you about my father. Impressive and daunting as he was, he didn't scare me – for he was my father. It would have grieved him to think that my childlike awe and respect for him made me see him as "too busy for me" or "too caught up in important things to care about my little stuff." Every loving father feels that way about his children.

So we can be sure that God wants us to come to his throne of grace. He is our Father! And by the good offices of his one perfect Son, our prayers will be made effective and powerful. As our high priest, Jesus has carried blood – not that of a sacrificial animal but his very own – to the mercy seat. He has presented himself in the very presence of God on our behalf to plead our case. He understands our case because he has lived our weaknesses and experienced the same trials and temptations we face. Our high priest is a real human being, our friend, our kinsman – yet without sin.

"Ah, but that 'without sin' business bothers me," someone says. "If he never yielded to sin, he doesn't know how horrible sin *really* is. It is only when you sin and feel the despair, forsakenness, and anguish of what you have done that the real weight of guilt comes crashing down on you!"

But, no. *No!* The power of Jesus to resist temptation means that Satan assaulted him with a ferocity you and I have never felt. When we yield, the pressure relents. For Jesus, the very endurance of temptation at the decibel-level it would have had in assaulting him would have involved suffering of a magnitude we cannot even imagine.

Then, in his experience on the cross, the one who had endured and resisted such terrible pressure nevertheless had the full weight of sin's despair, forsakenness, and anguish focused on him in laser-beam fashion. The one Perfect Son of God who was utterly without sin was treated as if he were the very embodiment of sin (cf. 2 Cor 5:21). He tasted of hell that day and was subjected to a greater terror and sense of loss than sin has ever brought one of us. He literally cried aloud, "My God, my God, why have you forsaken me!" (Matt 27:46).

The Credentials of Our High Priest

One cannot take the role of high priest to himself. It must be conferred. So the writer of Hebrews moves quickly to make it clear that the One seated on the throne has himself credentialed and ordained Jesus to his unique high priesthood. When he ascended "through the heavens" after his bodily resurrection, he was paving the way for us. He was not only opening heaven's door but was being declared, in his very person, "The Way." Because this is so, we do not have to face down Satan ourselves. We simply "hold firmly to the faith we profess" in the Christ who has already defeated him for our sake.

Every high priest is selected from among men and is

appointed to represent them in matters related to God, to offer
gifts and sacrifices for sins. He is able to deal gently with those
who are ignorant and are going astray, since he himself is
subject to weakness. This is why he has to offer sacrifices for
his own sins, as well as for the sins of the people.

No one takes this honor upon himself; he must be called by
God, just as Aaron was. So Christ also did not take upon himself
the glory of becoming a high priest. But God said to him,

> "You are my Son;
> Today I have become your Father."
> And he says in another place,
> "You are a priest forever,
> in the order of Melchizedek" (5:1-6).

Just as Aaron was selected and called to his role as Israel's
first high priest, so Jesus was selected and called to his high-
priestly function. Yet, just as Jesus is greater than angels,
Moses, and Joshua, he is also a greater high priest than Aaron.
His priesthood is "in the order of Melchizedek" – a phrase
that occurs no less than five times in Hebrews and so must be
important. It is such an important fact that our preacher will
treat the issue at some length later. For now, he simply tantalizes
his readers-hearers by dropping the mysterious name. For now,
he only hints at the "forever" significance to Christ's high
priesthood in this special order.

So Why the Distress?

If God does know and care, why is life so hard? If the
throne of mercy is open to us, why do so many of our prayers
go unanswered? If Christ is our high priest, why aren't our
petitions getting through? If he really is sympathetic, why
do the pressures of temptation and persecution still come
against believers?

These are real rather than hypothetical questions for
Christians in every generation. Do you recall how passionately
this church prayed for little Bailey Hall when that bullet crashed
through his skull and snarled the wiring in his brain? Don't you
remember how we pleaded for God to spare the life of Mark

Burress from cancer? And aren't you aware that 15-year-old Josh Wallen died last week – in spite of the fact that so many of you were praying for him, that Jeff and Becky poured our their hearts to God for their little boy, that some of us prayed over him in ICU and begged for him to recover? Somebody needs to make sense of this sort of thing for us! And the preacher does just that by reminding us of Jesus' own experience when he was enfleshed among us.

During the days of Jesus' life on earth, he offered up prayers and petitions with loud cries and tears to the one who could save him from death, and he was heard because of his reverent submission. Although he was a son, he learned obedience from what he suffered and, once made perfect, he became the source of eternal salvation for all who obey him and was designated by God to be high priest in the order of Melchizedek (5:7-10).

In his physical limitations and with his human fears, Jesus "offered up prayers and petitions with loud cries and tears to the one who could save him from death." Most scholars agree that the reference here is to the Gethsemane ordeal. Jesus knew what lay ahead for him the next day. As he anticipated having what I have already called the "full weight of sin" come crushing down on him, he shuddered. As he anticipated the separation from his Beloved Father, he cringed! (Although some scholars debate whether Jesus could have *really* pulled back from his purpose at this late date, why question it? If pulling back was impossible, the tears and pleas were *mock*-tears and *pretend*-pleas. If here and elsewhere his temptations did not entail the authentic possibility of yielding, then it is simply false to say "we have one who has been tempted in every way, just as we are.")

But doesn't the text say that Jesus "was heard" when he prayed those pitiful prayers? Yes, it does. *But he died the very next day! So why in the world would our preacher say God "heard" his petitions?*

God could have saved Jesus from death by either of two ways that occur to my mind: (1) by sparing him the *experience of death* on a Roman cross the next day or (2) by saving him from *bondage to death* as his everlasting fate. Jesus was certainly aware of these two possibilities for answering his prayer – and was praying, I think, for the former rather than the latter on that horrible night. But he ended his three times of intense prayer – so intense that sweat poured off his body as though he were bleeding – with reverent submission. By saying "Not my will but yours be done," he was essentially committing to obey the Father even if his obedience meant still more anguish and suffering. And it did! Gethsemane gave way to Calvary.

If we go back to Hebrews 2:14-18 for a moment, the same thing has already been said in slightly different words. In his oneness with God's creatures who have flesh and blood, he faced the devil's ultimate threat to human beings – the fear of death. Like us, he trembled. Like us, he cried out for relief. Unlike some of us, however, he knew that the death of the body was reversible. He knew that his Father could raise him from the dead and restore his life.

God "heard" the cries of Jesus – both from Gethsemane's garden and from Golgotha's tree – and delivered him from the stranglehold of death. By raising his body from the tomb on Sunday morning, heaven signaled that the human race need never again live as captives "held in slavery by their fear of death."

Jesus learned obedience by trusting the Father to see him through that ordeal. His reverent submission perfected him for his role as trail-blazer and trail-paver for us. In his perfection, he has become the source of eternal salvation for all who ever follow him on the obedient path of reverent submission. For our preacher-writer and his hearers-readers in the first century and for you and me, here is the offer: *Follow Jesus with the same reverent submission he showed the Father, and you will experience the same outcome.* Just as his faithful obedience under trial was part of the process that perfected him within God's greater plan, so is our faithful obedience under trial part of the process of purification and refinement for our faith.

There is a critical distinction that needs to be made here. Torture and death for Jesus was *never* the will of his Father. His will was our salvation, and the only route to that end required Calvary as its means. We can also say that insecurity, illness, or persecution for faith is *never* the will of the Father for us. His will is our salvation from an environment that has been cursed by sin and redemption from our own personal experiences of sin. But the only route to that end requires obedience – obedience that sometimes promises only further pain or greater persecution – as its means.

This is a hard truth of the Christian religion. In our fallen, selfish natures, we would much prefer to pray for things that will bring immediate pleasure, immediate relief from struggle. But we have committed to live for the long-term above the short-term, for spiritual above carnal, for the sake of fellowship with our Holy God who lies in unapproachable light above acceptance by those who are still captive to Satan and are living in darkness.

"Because [Jesus] himself suffered when he was tempted, he is able to help those who are being tempted" (2:18). So why would the preacher's first-century hearers try to face their temptations in their own human strength? With their Melchizedekan high priest identified, ordained, and forever at their disposal, why would they struggle with their personal stresses or external tormentors without his aid? He was able to help them!

Before we get too critical of our first-century brothers and sisters, perhaps we should look at ourselves very carefully. Why would *we* try to face *our* temptations in *our* limited human strength? I am grateful for physicians, lawyers, therapists, and teachers. I am especially grateful for them when they are compassionate and sensitive Christians. They can often fulfill the biblical duty of helping bear another's burdens (cf. Gal 6:2). But these offices and functions – even when performed by the godliest of persons – must never be the alternative to strength, guidance, and compassion from the Great High Priest of our profession. They are not enough. They fall devastatingly short of the aid Christ alone can give and is eager to provide.

Conclusion

In the final few days of Mark Burress' life, he repeatedly assured those of us who were privileged to be with him that he was so grateful for our constant prayers for him and his family. "They have been answered!" he said again and again.

"Hold on, Rubel!" somebody says. "Didn't he die last

month?" Yes. In Christ. At peace. And with the assurance that though he had not escaped the experience of death, he need have no fear of being in bondage to its power. Just like his high priest before him at the end of his own suffering, Mark will rise from the dead. And by his reverent submission through his three-year ordeal, he gave strength to his family, he taught his teachers, and he matured into a tower of spiritual strength and inspiration to many people.

The same process worked in the life of young Josh Wallen. Born with handicaps that had required surgery after surgery, the eight-hour operation he had a week ago Friday turned out to be the last one he could endure. He won't get a driver's license or graduate from high school or have grandchildren for Jeff and Becky. But that 15-year-old Christian boy adopted these verses from 2 Corinthians 12 in *The Message* as something of a motto by which he lived:

> I quit focusing on the handicap and began appreciating the gift. It was a case of Christ's strength moving in on my weakness. Now I take limitations in stride, and with good cheer, these limitations that cut me down to size – abuse, accidents, opposition, bad breaks. I just let Christ take over! And so the weaker I get, the stronger I become.

That's exactly what happened with Josh.

It is heaven's promise to Christians. We are the only ones with a Great High Priest who sympathizes because he has been where we are. On the strength of his intercession and by the power of his blood, we go to the throne of mercy with boldness. We go with the knowledge in advance that we will be heard. Whether we are spared the trial altogether, rescued from its clutches when it is about to snuff out our physical lives, or raised from the dead in triumph over it, we have his promise that nothing can destroy us.

So let us hold firmly to the faith we have professed. After all, we are not homeless paupers seeking a loan at the bank. We are not bankrupt folk trying to buy a car. We are not suppliants applying for documents through a corrupt bureaucracy. And if everyone else sees us as bewildered souls in a King's Palace who need a Prime Minister or High Priest to get us a hearing at the throne, we know better. We are beloved-but-beleaguered children in our Father's house – with our Big Brother carrying us to him in his powerful, loving arms.

9

We Are At Risk!

Hebrews 5:11—6:20

Rubel Shelly and John York
Woodmont Hills Church of Christ,
Nashville, Tennessee

Introduction

Luke Johnson points to the theme of suffering in the Hebrews sermon. The typical Christian reader of this material can more easily grasp that suffering was necessary for Jesus in his human experience than for him or her! This sermon is designed to draw out the truth that what was necessary for Jesus is also necessary for his followers. Our moral-spiritual transformation is accomplished through the very experiences that we least desire. In the course of this sermon, preached as a dialogue between John and Rubel, a young mother whose child was struck in the temple by a stray bullet approximately three years earlier and whose neurological state is severely impaired, speaks very candidly of the struggle that trauma introduced into her life. Note: The phrases in bold print in the sermon's conclusion indicate John and Rubel speaking alternately.

.

We Are at Risk!

Rubel Shelly: The watershed text of Hebrews came before us – in my opinion, at least – last Lord's Day. Here are the words: "Although [Jesus] was a son, he learned obedience from what he suffered and, once made perfect, he became the source of eternal salvation for all who obey him and was designated by God to be high priest in the order of Melchizedek" (5:8-10).

I think everything prior to those three verses which had claimed superiority for Jesus over angels, Moses, Joshua, and Aaron, was mere prelude to the great Christological confession of the perfection, saving power, and eternal high priesthood of the Lord Jesus Christ. The remainder of this sermon-epistle pulsates from this text. Specifically, discouraged and weak believers were exhorted to take heart from their leader. Just as he was perfected through suffering, so would they have to follow his lead. They should not be surprised at stress, opposition, or persecution. To the contrary, they should expect it. Am I right?

John York: I agree with you on both counts! Verses 8-10 of chapter five are critical to the preacher's understanding of both the humanity and divinity of Jesus. He believes that the suffering experienced in earthly life by Jesus taught him how to be the Perfect Son. It is thus reasonable to expect that the same learning devices would hold true for the rest of us.

Rubel: So what do you think our preacher-writer would think of the "gospel of health and wealth" that so many people hear from Christian pulpits and televangelists today?

John: I suppose he might have one of two reactions: either he would smile at what he considered a rather childish belief system that could be so foreign to the life of Jesus himself, or he would react like the prophets of old and level a shotgun blast against the self-centered materialism that wants to substitute human success stories for the gospel.

Rubel: What you're saying reminds me of some quotes I saw published a while back from comment cards turned in at Bridger Wilderness Area in the Teton National Forest of Wyoming. Remember now, this is a "wilderness" area. You would presume rough terrain, right? You would presume difficult hiking, right? Here's what people wrote:

"Too many rocks in the mountains."
"Trails need to be reconstructed. Please avoid building trails that go uphill."
"Trails need to be wider so people can walk while holding hands."
"Escalators would help on steep uphill sections."
"Chair lifts need to be in some places so that we can get to wonderful views without having to hike to them."

John: Whoa! That last one sounds like some of us Christians whining to God about our spiritual growth! *God, we want you to get us to the mountain peaks without expecting us to climb – or sweat!* If there is a recurring reality in the life of the early church, it is not that life suddenly becomes free of pain and suffering upon accepting Christ. Rather, the expectation is that his followers will share in his suffering.

In the ancient world there was a common saying: "To suffer is to learn." Obviously the proverb can be reversed: "To learn is to suffer." I'm reminded of the first day I tried snow skiing. I mastered the beginner's slope pretty quickly, so my uncle took me on the ski lift to the top of the mountain. I thought I would never get back down! After what seemed like hours of falling on both hips until they were blue, I looked at my uncle with that look – you know, "I'm done now!" He smiled and looked back and said, "Be patient. If you're not falling down, you're not learning anything."

Rubel: How do we get our heads around this concept? Maybe we need to post around this assembly hall for Christians what I hear is posted in lots of gyms: *No pain, no gain!*

John: Even so, we may need to qualify even that. Pain doesn't guarantee gain. It only gives the opportunity for it.

Rubel: Quite so! Pain is sometimes enough to make people quit. Give up. Indict God for his cruelty. Or even to curse him. I can admire Job without wanting to live his experience of economic reversal, the death of his children, and excruciating physical suffering! Far be it from any one of us to be too arrogant in telling in advance how he or she would handle one or more of these awful blows. And far be it from us to be too quick to judge or censure someone whose knees buckle under pressure.

John: Our teacher knew this was a difficult lesson to grasp. So, in the first section of today's text, he says:

> We have much to say about this, but it is hard to explain because you are slow to learn. In fact, though by this time you ought to be teachers, you need someone to teach you the elementary truths of God's word all over again. You need milk, not solid food! Anyone who lives on milk, being still an infant, is not acquainted with the teaching about righteousness. But solid food is for the mature, who by constant use have trained themselves to distinguish good from evil (5:11-14).

Our preacher becomes the scolding parent at this point, attempting to shame his audience into a better performance. It's not unlike the coach whose players have just had a miserable first half and he wants to shake them out of their lethargy by telling them that a grade school team could play better than that. The Hebrews writer's concern is that they should have become such a supportive community of faith that they didn't need him to tell them how to deal with their circumstances. They should be teaching one another at this point, but they still required teaching from the outside. They should be mature, complete in their spiritual support of one another, not children still nursing at the breast. Their constancy with God and his Word should mean constancy in their commitments, rather than the wavering and doubt they are experiencing.

Rubel: So here comes the challenge:

> Therefore let us leave the elementary teachings about Christ and go on to maturity, not laying again the foundation of repentance from acts that lead to death, and of faith in God, instruction about baptisms, the laying on of hands, the resurrection of the dead, and eternal judgment. And God permitting, we will do so (6:1-3).

Rather than wait for an escalator to take you to the high peaks of faith, start climbing. Instead of griping about the lack of a chair lift, imitate Jesus, your leader. Instead of staying an infant on milk for your entire Christian life, grow up – by chewing on solid food and exercising your spiritual muscles in Spirit-led discernment.

It is far too simplistic to say this is a challenge for Christians to advance beyond reading the Four Gospels and Acts so that we are finally reading Hebrews, Romans, and Revelation. That isn't what our teacher means by distinguishing "milk" from "meat." We "leave the elementary teachings about Christ" only in the sense that we move beyond those initial doctrines about repentance and faith that called us to baptismal commitment and laying-on-of-hands blessing and commissioning. We shoulder our burdens, bear the heat of the day, and hold firmly to our profession of faith in the face of whatever trials come to us. We have, in fact, been taught that we will someday be raised from the dead and rewarded for whatever sufferings we have had to endure at the final Great Day.

I think it is particularly interesting that our preacher does not entertain for a moment the idea that this is a lift-yourself-by-your-bootstraps philosophy. It has nothing to do with works righteousness or being worthy of salvation. It is simply following the normal and expected course of walking in the footsteps of Jesus – and being perfected or matured in the process. The English reading is a bit misleading here. "Let us go on to maturity" is more literally "let us be *carried to* maturity." In other words, creating Christlike character in a disciple is less our willpower than his Spirit-empowerment, less our strength than his, and less our accomplishment than his gift.

John: Anyone who doesn't see the challenge of enduring, holding on, and being willing to suffer for Christ isn't being realistic. That is why it is so false for people to leave the impression that being a Christian makes life easier. What we called health-and-wealth gospel is false gospel that sets people up to be destroyed. We begin to believe that living the American dream of health, wealth, success, and long life are almost owed to us because we're good church-goers. When it doesn't work that way – and it never does, even when it appears that way from a distance – then we begin to discover the importance of our faith and our community of faith.

Life isn't fair! Every prayer for healing isn't answered the way we would like. Every desire for the perfect job isn't met. Job losses happen. Those we love die before we're ready. Yes, we celebrate the victories; we celebrate those obvious moments when tragedy is overcome, when addictions are beaten, when success is celebrated as a gift from God. We also recognize that Jesus learned obedience through what he suffered, not through the success of his miracles. What a testimony we receive when Mark Burress says that his prayers were answered even in his death or Jeff and Becky Wallen stand at the memorial service of their son and announce they will give God praise even in the midst of their sorrow and pain.

Rubel: John, Terry Smith and I were having a conversation with another of those people in our church whose struggle has been very public and whose ordeal seems to be unrelenting. She was voicing her frustrations. She trusted us enough to tell us how angry and sad she sometimes felt. And she said something to this effect: "But, of course, I can't say that out loud at church!"

I cut her off at that point – not to suggest that she had said something inappropriate that called for scolding, but to say that I thought it might be a good idea for her to do just that. Not every faith story ends in quick victory. Not every Daniel who gets thrown into a den of lions gets out without a scratch. There are lots of bones in those dens! So, Jennifer Stewart, would you come up here with John and me? Would you be willing to tell this church how you have felt lately?

Jennifer Stewart: Just over three weeks ago, I was on my way to work, as had become the usual since beginning my nursing career in February. I had grown accustomed to going to work, coming home, making things, fixing things, doing things – filling up my spare time with just about anything I could to make myself feel useful, to prove to myself that I was always doing something of importance, to avoid facing the feelings that I have managed to suppress most often quite convincingly, at least I like to believe, for the last several years. But this night was different. And I know why that was.

In an argument with a friend earlier that day, I was told that I needed to seek counseling, I needed to be medicated – that I had lost it. He could tell that I'm just not myself anymore. It's funny how sometimes you can grow so angry with someone for making a comment such as that based solely on your belief that they couldn't be more wrong. However, more times than not, I think being confronted with the truth is what hurts so much more, because sometimes they couldn't be more right. He was right. And as angry and hurt as I was that someone could believe that of me, I was absolutely astonished and totally unprepared to face the fact that I could have ever let myself get here, that at such a young age I had let life get the best of me. Yet, at the same time, in a way I was so very thankful that he had both the ability to recognize that, and even more, the courage to let me know that he did.

I stopped right in front of the hospital, five minutes from the start of my shift, literally crying so hard that I couldn't see the stoplight in front of me turning green. I knew that there was no way that I could possibly collect myself enough to walk through those doors and hold a child's life in my hands. The hypocrisy of holding a career founded on the preciousness of life when all I really wanted was an end to my life—I just couldn't fake it anymore. I picked up the phone, without knowing whom to call, without believing anyone would care, and immediately found myself dialing Terry Smith's number. I'm still uncertain as to how he managed to understand a word I said, as I cried uncontrollably for the entire conversation. But somehow he knew all that he needed to know – that I needed a friend. And that is what has led me here today.

I understand that I have lost it. I, not anyone else. I have chosen the path that my life has taken. The decisions that I have made, situations and relationships that I have either placed myself in, or stupidly removed myself from, I could have avoided. I have pushed away so many people that cared, people who tried to support me, until I finally reached a point that I felt I had no right to ask for more. And what I chose to perceive as being abandoned was simply my way of rationalizing the isolation in which I had placed myself.

What it is that I have lost is simple. It's hope – the hope

that I will one day see my son walk, or hear him laugh. That I will see him off for his first day of school or stay up all night worrying when he's on a date at 16 and stays out too late. That anyone will ever know how wonderful he is, and what he could have been. The hope that everything he suffers through, all the teasing and stares and being left out, isn't for naught, because if I can't believe in a God who would allow this, then I can't very well believe that there's a better life after this one. And the most wretched feeling of guilt that results from the hope that the next time he enters the hospital, he won't leave, not because I don't love him, but because I do. That's the hardest thing I have ever had to admit, not just to you, but to myself. Because I would trade places with him in a heartbeat. I have lost the feeling that I have control, because the one thing I want to change is out of my hands, and I don't know how to deal with that. I've lost the feeling that I belong, not just here, but anywhere. That I deserve to be loved. That I can fall down knowing that someone is there to catch me, no matter how badly I screwed up. That I can fail, and it's OK. The strength to carry the load that both life and myself have managed to pile up. But even more tragic, it's the will to want to.

But most importantly I have found in the last few weeks through meeting with both Terry and Rubel, I have *lost* it. It's not destroyed, not forever gone. It's simply beyond my grasp right now. I can't do it alone. I know that now. And even better, I know it's OK to say that. And that's part of the reason I am here. I realize I am only one of the many people sitting here today with a broken heart. There isn't one of us whose life is any less important than another. And despite the fact that over the last few weeks I have begun to find hope again, and because of that, knowing how easy it would be to go on acting as if I am as strong, as I have pretended to be for so long now, I felt it the right thing to do, to show the real me, at my worst, hoping that by doing so, any of you who are hurting can know that you are not alone. I owe that to my children, to you, but most of all to myself: to prove that there is no shame in letting everyone else see inside your heart. I need help. But more than anything, I need to know that I, that any of us, can come to each other to say that. To know that we are all in this life together.

I need to know that neither money nor distance nor bloodlines – nothing separates us. To remind myself that we are all children of God. We are all a family. And that when one of us has lost our way, the rest of us will do anything to bring that person back. I have to believe that. And I thank you so much for affording me to opportunity to open up and finally begin to heal – from the inside out.

John: If church isn't a safe enough place for someone to voice these frustrations and pains, where is such a place? So often we start believing that only the good endings can be spoken at church. Only the completed success stories can be offered up to God. But that is the reality of *lament* in Scripture and in our lives, isn't it? This is precisely what the preacher of Hebrews wanted from his audience. He wanted them to tell one another their stories and then hold one another up; hold each other in accountability and commitment in the name of Jesus. So, Rubel, in the face of something as real and personal to this church as what Jennifer has just said, what can a sermon series from Hebrews do for us? Is the preaching just scolding us and telling us to buck up? Or is there more to it than that?

Rubel: If it *can't* help Jennifer or the Burresses or the Wallens or the rest of us with our struggles, we should find something that will! But what John and I believe, church, is that our preaching each week is set in the context of your economic stress, your marital problems, your bereavement, your doubts – and must bring a word from God to those situations. If we didn't think the best way to help you was through Scripture, we'd just play tapes of Oprah and Dr. Phil on the big screen! For whatever insights of value you can get from psychology, group support, or a loving church, you ultimately need a word from God Almighty himself that will get you through.

John: And although the tradition of conservative churches such as ours is to stress the language of 6:4-12 about the possibility of spiritual apostasy, the thrust of this text is not negative. It does not seek to scare people about the fate they will suffer if they abandon Christ. This preacher's goal is positive. He believes the best about his friends and spiritual family – and wants them to be encouraged.

Sometimes we lift verses 4-8 out of context and become

consumed with our modern question of whether or not saved
people can be lost. But if you listen to the words in the larger
context, he has no interest in any of his believing audience
losing their salvation. Yes, no one should neglect the great
salvation that God has given in Jesus. Yes, if one rejects that
salvation, either initially or especially after already receiving it,
there are no alternative means of entering into God's presence.
If we reject Jesus as Lord and reject the participation of the Holy
Spirit in our lives, God doesn't have any other avenues into his
presence. But that reminder is all for the purpose of reminding
his audience of the gift they have received. Whatever the world
around them may be saying about their newfound faith in Jesus,
they need to trust God – not those empty voices. Listen to the
preacher's assurances regarding his listening audience:

> Even though we speak like this, dear friends, we are
> confident of better things in your case – things that
> accompany salvation. God is not unjust; he will not
> forget your work and the love you have shown him as
> you have helped his people and continue to help them.
> We want each of you to show this same diligence to
> the very end, in order to make your hope sure. We
> do not want you to become lazy, but to imitate those
> who through faith and patience inherit what has been
> promised (6:9-12).

His focus is on the positive outcome of their communal
commitments to Christ and to one another. This is a
"ya'll-project," not an individual endurance contest. The
diligence and hope that sustain come through their communal
efforts to support one another.

Rubel: Precisely! And these strong words of encouragement
are rooted in the history of God's dealings with humankind
across the centuries. In Hebrews 11, our writer will tick off
a long list of names. God kept his promise to every one of
those people! Here he cites only one example. His example is
Abraham, the Father of all those who have faith in God.

Abraham's life was a series of winding treks from Ur to
Egypt, through Sodom and Shur – and he died never having

inherited Canaan. Along the way, both he and Sarah laughed at the notion of a child in their old age. They even attempted surrogate motherhood with Hagar. Oh, the heartache that started! It was a long, tough, and painful journey. But Abraham was encouraged every step of the way, so our preacher says, by God's "promise" vouchsafed to him. And that promise was rooted in two things. First, it was backed by God's very character, his "unchanging nature." Second, it was confirmed to Abraham by a covenant "oath" that was passed from Abraham to his heirs.

Now God has done a similar thing with Christians: "God did this so that, by two unchangeable things in which it is impossible for God to lie, we who have fled to take hold of the hope offered to us may be greatly encouraged. We have this hope as an anchor for the soul, firm and secure" (6:18-19a). The same God who swore by his unchanging character to Abraham has made a covenant promise to all of us who have put our faith in Jesus Christ, and has further reinforced that covenant by making Jesus our eternal high priest who is even today functioning in the true Holy of Holies on our behalf (6:19b-20).

John: Here is what today's text means, then, to all the Jennifer Stewarts of this church and to the entire family of God, to all of us who ever feel like we're losing it. It means that we're all in this together! It means we uphold one another precisely in the difficult times. To learn is to suffer; to suffer is to learn. Jesus grew back into his divine Sonship and was restored to the throne room of God in exactly the same way that God grows his divine nature in us and promises to bring us into that same heavenly realm. He does not leave us on our own, but calls us into relationship. Yes, those basic teachings that are our initial experiences of God's salvation – our repentance and baptism and our belief that Jesus really was raised from the dead – need to be remembered. But we also have to help each other get through the painful training that is shaping us for eternity. It's not easy. It's not fair. Much of it comes without warning or provocation, and we can't survive it alone. Thus, Jesus himself endured it so he could plead our cause before God, even as we cry out to God and to one another.

Rubel: Let us close with a final observation about a play on words in today's text. Our teacher opens at 5:11 with a tongue-in-cheek comment about how "slow" (Gk, *nuthros* means sluggish) some of his students seemed to be and returns to the same word and theme at 6:12. In the second reference, however, he is actually voicing his confidence that they will not be "lazy" but faithful to their confession. And what had stung them awake from their sluggishness? Suffering! It makes weak Christians see just how desperately we need the strength of the Holy Spirit. In our weakness, we are able to sense his power at work (cf. 2 Cor 12:7ff).

Again, however, I hasten to add that his strong confidence is not so much in them but in the certain promises God has made them. He is not about to abandon them in their crisis moments – even if there is no rescue from their suffering except through death and resurrection in a new heaven and earth. But God will not abandon them to the enemy. He will not allow anything to destroy their spiritual security.

We are at risk because Satan is intent on seducing us into evil; if he cannot do that, he will try to deceive us with the false doctrine that the negative things that happen in our lives are "acts of God." We are at risk because life is hard; we sometimes cry out in our spiritual immaturity and indict God as a tormenter – something Job, for example, refused to do. We are at risk because our faith is weak; we need to press on from the elementary teachings about Jesus into the lifestyle of trust, submission, and obedience he modeled for us – even though that lifestyle invites suffering for the sake of righteousness. We are at risk because there is so much about living as human beings that is simply mysterious and defies explanation within our limited theological frameworks or personal insights.

Because we are at risk, we must believe. *Believe* that God is still on his throne, in spite of the terrible things sin has introduced into his cosmos. *Believe* that the God who cannot lie will keep his promise of deliverance – even if that deliverance comes only in the resurrection. *Believe* that our Melchizedekan high priest, who sympathizes with our predicament, has secured our redemption by blood and is interceding for us constantly at the mercy seat. *Believe* that the things through which we persevere in faith not only cannot destroy us but will serve to mature us, perfect us, form the image of Christ in us.

No matter what is threatening you today, you are challenged to believe. To endure. To suffer in hope. To look beyond the temporal to the eternal. To share his triumph at his appearing and kingdom. We are so confident of Jennifer, Ken and Ginger, Melanie and Gracie, and Jeff, Becky, and Jessie that we would like to close with our own expanded paraphrase of Hebrews 6:9-12.

John and Rubel reading together: **We are so confident of God's ability to work in you** – and of your demonstrated willingness to trust him through the dark circumstances of life on Planet Earth – **that we believe the sort of steadfast faith that accompanies salvation will continue to be exhibited in this church.** Our duty to one another is mutual support within this faith community, to be there for one another in trying times. **God is not unjust, and he will not allow any of us to be tempted above what we can bear!** No, he will help us as we help one another. **And you may be absolutely confident that he will see you through to the end.** He will validate your hope with the elation of triumph – **even if, as in the case of his Beloved Son, the triumph comes after apparent defeat!** So don't get lazy, sluggish, or careless in your faith – **especially if things are going well for you today.** Don't think for a moment that your time will not come. **But know that God will be there in advance of your trial and will do for you what he did for Abraham, Joseph, and the thousands of others who persevered through faith.** We will inherit all he has promised to those who love him. *We have his word on it!*

10

Did Anything Happen?

Hebrews 12:18-29

James W. Thompson

Abilene Christian University, Abilene, Texas

Introduction

James teaches New Testament and Preaching courses at Abilene Christian University. He has published a number of works on Hebrews, including a monograph for Catholic Biblical Quarterly entitled *The Beginnings of Christian Philosophy*. Preachers also consider his book, *Strategy for Survival*, a valuable resource as they consider preaching from Hebrews. James offers the following context for this sermon:

> The sermon text reflects my life-long journey with Hebrews, a journey that began with my doctoral dissertation, which focused on Heb. 12:18-29. The sermon grows out of the interaction between my reading of the text and the questions raised in congregational life. Specifically, I have increasingly heard of calls for worship renewal, which appeared to presuppose that the quality of our worship depends on our own creativity. In response to multiple messages of this kind, I returned to Hebrews and imagined that the passage is a response to people whose interest in worship had declined as the readers saw nothing in their house churches that compared with the excitement offered by other religions. This comparison

led me to ask, "Did anything happen?" The text from Hebrews indicates that "something happens," even if it is not apparent to the senses.

Though by no means the only one in this volume, this sermon demonstrates one principle that Charles Campbell discusses in his chapter. A sub narrative lies behind the discursive form of the Hebrews letter. This sermon assumes the sub narrative of Israel's history and offers a discursive interpretation of that history through the lens of Hebrews 12: 18-29. The sermon also exemplifies the quality of "movement" or "journey" that Richard Eslinger describes a good sermon possessing.

Did Anything Happen?

The first church service recorded in the Bible was also the greatest one, and no one would ever forget it. The scene of Israel gathered at Mount Sinai was the first assembly, and no assembly after it would match the impact that it had. The Israelites remembered that moment forever in their songs and stories. Here was the moment when they received the Ten Commandments. But it was more than that. Our ancestors assembled to hear the word of the Lord, but more happened that day than they ever could have anticipated. The Lord came down in fire and smoke. There was the blast of the trumpet, the clouds and the thunder. It was such a terrifying scene that Moses said, "I tremble with fear." That was quite a church service. Something happened that put the listeners in awe.

There were other moments like this—overpowering moments. Moses encounters God at the burning bush, and he will never be the same. A few centuries later Isaiah enters the temple. He sees the Lord sitting on a throne, high and lofty; and the hem of his robe fills the temple. Seraphs sing, "Holy, holy, holy is the Lord of hosts. The whole earth is full of his glory." Isaiah responds, Woe is me...." It was quite a church service. Something happened that was unforgettable, and it changed his life.

The centuries have passed, and we still assemble before the same Lord. In fact, the most obvious thing we do is to assemble. We have never had an experience quite like that of the Israelites at Mount Sinai or Isaiah in the temple, but we have had moments when something happened, and we were moved by the experience. For many of us, it is the blending of voices together in harmony. I still remember the first time I heard the singing at the old Sewell auditorium at ACU. We thought we were hearing angelic voices. We may have had our own "mountaintop experiences." We had moments when we, like those before us, were moved by the experience of worship. It might have been a moment of worship under the stars. Or at an occasion when the sermon spoke to us; or at a time when we could appreciate the beauty of God's creation. We were not at Mount Sinai, but we have been present in worship when something happened.

The reality is, however, that worship is not always like that. We do not always find our pulse quickening, and we do not always have the experience of Israel at Sinai or Isaiah in the temple. We do not always say, with Moses, "I tremble with fear." No one can repeat mountaintop experiences week after week. People are assembling around the world today—in stately Gothic churches, in houses, in storefronts, and in mud huts with straw roofs. They do what Christians have done for centuries: they read the Bible, share in the Lord's Supper, sing, and pray. The style of worship may vary from culture to culture, but some things are always the same. Sometimes the setting is not very pleasing aesthetically, and often they cannot retreat into air conditioned churches where they can seal off the distractions of the outside world. No one confuses their singing with angelic voices, nor their worship with Mount Sinai. Nothing seems to happen.

We face a critical problem in our own affluent and entertainment- saturated world. The most pervasive issue among churches throughout North America is the question of what we can do with our assemblies. We come with very high expectations, but the fact that our services are predictable and unchanging creates problems for people who are accustomed to change. We can turn on our television and see dazzling special effects that leave us in awe and music that sounds angelic. We experience the drama and the passion of a football game, where electricity runs through the crowd. Here is awe. Then we ask about our assemblies, which can't match the movies for drama or the football stadium for enthusiasm. No wonder that some say that the football stadiums are the cathedrals of North America! Here, in the world of entertainment, something really happens to us.

But does anything happen in worship? We want desperately to recapture in worship that special "mountaintop experience" that we have glimpsed before. Our conversation turns toward how we can make something happen. An amazing number of articles and books are being published on what we can do about worship to make it more attractive and to ensure that something happens. We may work with the acoustics of our buildings, experiment with new worship forms, introduce new songs, and change the furniture of our house of worship—all in an effort to "do something" with worship.

It's a good thing to want to renew our worship. It's true that we can learn something about renewing the power of the worship. I know that many of us are looking for that experience that leaves us in awe. But I believe there is a missing dimension to the conversation. Today's text addresses this issue and reminds us that our problem is not entirely new. Long ago there was a little house church, probably in a major city. The members were showing signs of apathy, and some were not coming to the assemblies very regularly. The years had passed, and nothing had happened. They had experienced the enthusiasm at the beginning, but now the fire was going out. The assembly in the little house church could not compare with the sights and sounds of the world around them. The members knew about worship in the temple. It was filled with the pageantry of the priests in their ornate robes, the smell of incense, and the sounds of the choral music of the Levites. That was a church service! But all they had now was the little house church. One can doubt the professional qualities of those who led the worship services. Nothing seemed to be happening. Undoubtedly, the members could endure the trials of living in a hostile environment if only something happened in the assembly! They could meet the demands of living a Christian life and the stresses facing the community if only they could see something! But now the years had passed, and some of them were apparently asking if it was worth it to come to the assembly when nothing seemed to be happening.

To make matters worse, the listeners to the Letter to the Hebrews now faced hostile neighbors who discriminated against them and threatened their way of life. To face the struggle and weariness of the long pilgrimage with Jesus would be perfect if only they could see and feel something! If only the church service could be so overpowering they could know for sure that the struggle was worth it. I suspect that the author of Hebrews addressed his message to those who barely made it to worship.

The writer speaks a word of encouragement. And then he

writes: "You have not come to something that can be touched, a blazing fire, and darkness and gloom, and a tempest, and the sound of a trumpet, and a voice whose words made the hearers beg that no other word be spoken to them." No, we haven't come to repeat the remarkable experience of Sinai. Here in the assembly there is no thunder, no whirlwind. Here, where nothing seems to be happening, we have come to more than that. Here, in the house church, we have come to something that is greater than the first church service. For the ancient community, as for us, worship seems so ordinary with its endless routine.

But, says the author, "You have come to Mt. Zion, to the city of the living God, to the heavenly Jerusalem." In the house church—and in our assemblies—we have come to something greater than Sinai. Something is happening! Whether we feel our pulse race or not, whether you feel moved or not, we have come into the very presence of God. To meet with God's people is to encounter far more than we can touch or see. Despite what our senses tell us, our worship spans heaven and earth. In worship we encounter the invisible God. As the author of Hebrews says earlier in this sermon, "Faith is the assurance of things hoped for, the conviction of things not seen." Even when we see and feel nothing, we are in the presence of God.

The author of Hebrews does not say that something might happen when the professional performance matches our expectations. He does not say that something might happen because of our own creativity. "*You have come* to Mount Zion, the city of the living God...." The power of worship does not depend on us, but on the God who has come near in Jesus Christ.

We do not claim that we give no thought to giving our best in worship. Nor do we suggest that forms of worship do not change. But the fact is that we have come to Mount Zion, the heavenly Jerusalem. Our worship is not limited to this place.

To the assembly of twelve in a building meant for 300, he says, "You have come to Mount Zion, the heavenly Jerusalem."

To the assembly in a storefront that cannot escape the distractions of the city, he says, "You have come to Mount Zion."

To a house church in a tenth story apartment in a European city, he says, "You have come to Mount Zion."

To a tiny assembly of eight in a remote rural farming community, he says, "You have come to Mount Zion."

To an assembly of 700 or 1000 he says, "You have come to Mount Zion, the city of the living God."

Imagine what takes place here. We join in worship with the heavenly world. We are never limited to the house church or our own assembly. In worship we meet with the angels. In worship we come before God, who is the judge of all, and Christ, whose blood speaks to us. Something is really happening.

But worship is more than that. We worship with the universal church. We meet with the "church of the firstborn whose names are written in heaven." We join with the brothers and sisters throughout the world who share in the Lord's Supper on this day. In countless languages, they call on God. Some of you will recall brothers and sisters in Zambia and Kenya. When you share in the Lord's Supper, they are a part of your fellowship. Some of us will recall brothers and sisters in Singapore, Malaysia, and Thailand. Others will recall brothers and sisters in Buenos Aires, Rostov, and Haiti. Something is happening.

But worship is more than that. "You have come to the spirits of the just who have been made perfect." Worship is the occasion when we recall those who have gone before us-that great cloud of witnesses that we know through the Bible, and also the great cloud of witnesses who have shaped our faith. We join with Abraham, Isaac, and Jacob. We recall our own teachers in the faith—those who have completed their work. Worship is the occasion for joining with them.

And worship is more than that. You have come "to Jesus, the mediator of a new covenant, and to the sprinkled blood that speaks a better word than the blood of Abel." They heard the voice of God at Sinai. When we come to worship, we encounter the crucified Lord, who speaks to us more eloquently than the voice of Abel, "whose blood cried out." We may not hear the voice of God as it shook the earth at Sinai, but in worship we hear the voice of the Christ who addresses us in all circumstances. What an extraordinary experience!

Our temptation with any extraordinary experience is to become so accustomed to it that we no longer recognize or appreciate what we have. I sometimes wonder what it would be like to live in the Alps and to face the Matterhorn day after day; or to visit the Louvre so often as to become so familiar with Michelangelo's David as to no longer appreciate it; or to become so accustomed to the privileges of living in an affluent society with its material privileges that we no longer recognize what we have; or to miss the amazing privilege of meeting with the people of God in worship. The greatest of wonders easily become routine for us.

And when they become routine, we are tempted to think of this great privilege only in terms of what it does for us. We easily think of worship that way. But the author of Hebrews has a reminder that worship is not about us, for he says, "See that you do not refuse the one who is speaking." The God who provides these privileges is the one who summons us to recognize that he "is a consuming fire." To worship is to come in awe before the creator and judge. Worship is not about us, but about God! When we come before God, something happens.

11

No Enduring City

Hebrews 13:12-14

Ross Thomson
North Lake Church of Christ,
Atlanta, Georgia

Introduction

Born in Scotland, Ross brings a rich and diverse background to the pulpit. He has preached for the North Lake church near Atlanta since 1997. This sermon reflects theological insight and pastoral sensitivity in communicating a vital dimension of the message of the book of Hebrews.

Richard Eslinger highlights the tension in Hebrews between being grounded in the basic virtues of boldness, memory, and steadfast hope while at the same time traveling the journey. This sermon seeks to flesh out that tension by grounding Christians in the history of God's people at the same time stepping out in faith on the journey of discipleship.

No Enduring City

First Reading

By faith Abraham, when called to go to a place he would later receive as his inheritance, obeyed and went, even though he did not know where he was going. By faith he made his home in the promised land like a stranger in a foreign country; he lived in tents, as did Isaac and Jacob, who were heirs with him of the same promise. For he was looking forward to the city with foundations, whose architect and builder is God.

Hebrews 11:8-10

Second Reading

And so Jesus also suffered outside the city gate to make the people holy through his own blood. Let us, then, go to him outside the camp, bearing the disgrace he bore. For here we do not have an enduring city, but we are looking for the city that is to come.

Hebrews 13:12-14

By the Mississippi River, at the jumping-off point of the Lewis and Clark expedition, is a historical marker which reads, "From this place Lewis and Clark began the expedition into the Northwest Territory which opened up a new land of promise for those with the courage to claim it."

And men and women in modern America come and stand there and remember a time when the prairie schooners rolled across the plains, when American people were an armed camp of circled wagons surrounded by hostile enemies, when you could only dream of the great cities to come. Visitors come to the memorial and they are stirred by heroic images from the past and wonder, perhaps how they, too, might be a part of that great story which is America.

Likewise, the sermon called "Hebrews" stands as a historical marker, reminding us of that great story which is the kingdom of God, and exhorting us to play our part in it. The writer, throughout the whole book, but culminating in the

13th chapter, unites two things: history and faith. He takes the
most powerful symbols of the past and provides meaning for
the present. He flashes before us heroic images from the time
when Zion was nothing more than a wandering desert caravan,
an armed camp in the Sinai, homeless people living in tent
cities, with no place of their own but dreaming of the city to
come. And he asks us to step into that dream with them. The
city on a hill is one of the most powerful and enduring symbols
known to humankind; consider Zion in the Old Testament, the
glory of Athens, or the Eternal City of Rome on the seven hills.
This image was part of the founding vision of America. In 1630,
aboard the ship *Arabella*, John Winthrop, the future leader
of the Massachusetts Bay Colony, preached a sermon which,
in the words of Daniel Boorstin, "struck the keynote of
American history:"

> Wee shall be as a Citty upon a Hill, the eies of all
> people are uppon us; soe that if wee shall deale falsely
> with our God in this worke wee have undertaken and
> soe cause him to withdrawe his present help from us,
> wee shall be made a story and a by-word through
> the world.

Three hundred fifty years later, Ronald Reagan tapped into
that same sense of American destiny with his own "City on a
Hill" speech. He struck the same powerful chord, urging the
nation to strive again to be that city, to seek that promise. The
symbol of the city on a hill endures because the city is still the
stuff of dreams. It is a transcendent symbol of perfection. In this
world, perfection is always up ahead and we approach it only as
pilgrims. It is a heroic call and we are creatures who desire in
our deepest souls to be called to sacrifice for something bigger
than what already exists, to dream the impossible dream. Great
leaders have always called their people to that.

Tomorrow is Martin Luther King Day. Recall with me his
unforgettable call to the dream of a just society:

> I have a dream that one day every valley shall be
> exalted, every hill and mountain shall be made low.
> The rough places will be plain and the cooked places

will be made straight, "and the glory of the Lord shall be revealed, and all flesh shall see it together." This is our hope.

This is the faith that I go back to the South with. With this faith we will be able to hew out of the mountain of despair, a stone of hope. With this faith we will be able to transform the jangling discords of our nation into a beautiful symphony of brotherhood. With this faith we will be able to work together, to pray together, to struggle together, to go to jail together, to stand up for freedom together, knowing that we will be free one day.

So let freedom ring from the prodigious hilltops of New Hampshire. Let freedom ring from the mighty mountains of New York. Let freedom ring from the heightening Alleghenies of Pennsylvania. Let freedom ring from the snowcapped Rockies of Colorado. Let freedom ring from the curvaceous slopes of California.

But not only that. Let freedom ring from Stone Mountain of Georgia. Let freedom ring from Lookout Mountain of Tennessee. Let freedom ring from every hill and molehill of Mississippi. "From every mountainside, let freedom ring."

And when this happens, and when we allow freedom to ring, when we let it ring from every village and every hamlet, from every state and every city, we will be able to speed up that day when all of God's children, black men and white men, Jews and gentiles, Protestants and Catholics, will be able to join hands and sing in the words of the old Negro spiritual: "Free at last. Free at last. Thank God Almighty, we are free at last."

King went to the mountaintop and saw the Promised Land, but never entered it. He saw a Promised Land where love is triumphant, all people are brothers, and we are all one in Christ. None of us enter in this life, but that doesn't matter. What matters is that we live our lives as people on a journey, striving for a better world. It matters that we try. America's motto is on its banknotes: *E. Pluribus Unum*—"out of many, one"—a simple but profound motto, something worth living up to. Our congregation has a simple motto: To "make disciples of all people" ... "of all people."

Huckleberry Finn is a story about two outcasts—a poor white boy named Huck and a black slave named Jim. Jim is fleeing slavery and Huck's civilization. They travel at night down the Mississippi River and as they go down the river they get to know one another. They share their dreams. Jim's dream is to make enough money to buy his wife out of slavery and then for the two of them to save enough money to buy their own children. All through the journey, Jim looks after Huck... even taking his watch so he can sleep.

Huck is torn apart spiritually. On the one hand, this black man is his best friend. On the other, in the city of his birth, even in the religion of his childhood, Jim is a piece of property. According to civilized law he is 3/5 of a human being. Thus, Huck is racked with guilt over what is, in effect, his theft of another person's property. He is even tormented by the thought that he might be headed for hell.

Huck writes a letter of confession to Jim's owner, telling him what has happened and where they are. But he can't mail it. Then, in one of the most beautiful moments in literature, one night on his watch, Huck stares in agony into the blackness of the river. He holds the letter in his trembling hand, says to himself, "All right then, I'll go to hell," and tears it up.

Brothers and sisters, never forget that Jesus went to hell for us—all of us, of every race. The established religion—the religion of "civilization," respectability, conventional righteousness, and ceremony, had nothing for us. It still doesn't. "And so," the writer of Hebrews tells us, "Jesus also suffered outside the city gate to make the people holy through his own blood"(Heb 13:12). Jesus willingly died on a hill overlooking the burning fires of the city dump, looking into the Valley of Hinnon... Or, as we name it, Gehenna.

And so the preacher rallies us. "Let us, then, go to him outside the camp, bearing the disgrace he bore. For here we do not have an enduring city, but we are looking for the city that is to come" (Heb 13:13-14).

There are two words in Hebrew for "camp." One means "safe" (a sanctuary in the wilderness); the other means "sacred, holy, set apart." We humans always feel safest when the wagons are all circled. We like a nice, respectable, comfortable worship performance on Sunday; we like participating in a pleasurable way, in the ceremony, having our elevated thoughts. That's one view of holiness. Then there's the other kind, in the book of Hebrews, Jesus' brand. Hebrews shouts at us, "You are an army. Why does everything center around the barracks and petty things? Break camp; march; let go of everything comfortable and safe. Die. It's not about ceremony; it's about grace—grace for a lost world."

And the words of Jesus ring in our ears:

All authority in heaven and on earth has been given to me. Therefore go and make disciples of all nations, baptizing them in the name of the Father and of the Son and of the Holy Spirit, and teaching them to obey everything I have commanded you. And surely I am with you always, to the very end of the age
(Matt 28:18-20).

And we are fortified with the promise that if we go where He wants, "the gates of hell will not prevail" against us. Do you believe that? That is the vision we want to embrace here: a vision to "make disciples." That's what we want of our children's program, our youth program. We want adult education to be more than education: not merely academic, but classes in discipling. In our marriage seminars we want more than to have happy, functional marriages. We want marriages that will glorify God. As a church we want to go "outside the camp," with Jesus...beyond these walls, into all the world.

LaVergne, TN USA
17 March 2011
220497LV00002B/1/A